30 Days of Sex Talks
Empowering Your Child with Knowledge of Sexual Intimacy
For Ages 3-7

Educate and Empower Kids, LLC
© 2023 by Educate and Empower Kids

All rights reserved. Published 2023.

ISBN: 978-1-7367215-7-5

The paper used in this publication meets the minimum requirements of the American National Standard for Information Sciences—Permanence of Paper for Printed Library Materials, ANSI Z39.48-1992.

IF YOU ENJOYED THIS BOOK, PLEASE LEAVE A POSITIVE REVIEW ON AMAZON.COM

Thank you to the following people for their support of our 30 Days of Sex Talks projects
Ed Allison
Mary Ann Benson, MSW, LSW
Scott Hounsell
Cliff Park

For great resources and information, follow us.

Facebook: www.facebook.com/lds.eduempowerkids
Twitter: @EduEmpowerKids
Pinterest: @EmpowerLDSKids
Instagram: @EduEmpowerKids
www.educateempowerkids.org

Be sure to check out our accompanying video series for this book at educateempowerkids.org

To view or download the additional resources listed at the end of each lesson, please follow the link in this QR code.

Educate and Empower Kids would like to acknowledge the following people who contributed time, talents, and energy to this publication:

Dina Alexander, MS

Jenny Webb, MA
K. Parker
Miriam Foulke
Amanda Scott
Caron C. Andrews

Design and Illustration by:
Jera Mehrdad and Zachary Hourigan

30 Days of Sex Talks

Empowering Your Child with Knowledge of Sexual Intimacy

For AGES 3-7

30 DAYS OF SEX TALKS
TABLE OF CONTENTS

INTRODUCTION X

AGES 3-7

1. Our Amazing Bodies 1
2. My Body Belongs to Me 3
3. Male Anatomy 5
4. Female Anatomy 7
5. Respecting Others 9
6. Public 11
7. Private 13
8. Clothing 15
9. Good Touch 17
10. Bad Touch 19
11. Predators 23
12. How to Say No 27
13. Your Instincts Keep You Safe 29
14. You Have Feelings and Emotions that Connect You 31
15. Romantic Love 33
16. Adults Who Care for You 35
17. Where do Babies Come From? 37
18. We Change and Develop 41
19. Other Words You've Heard 45
20. Discovering Our Own Bodies 47
21. Affection 49
22. Play 53
23. How are Boys and Girls Alike? 55
24. Friendships 57
25. My Body Poops and Pees! 59
26. Pornography 61
27. Pictures 65
28. Phones and the Internet 69
29. Nudity 73
30. I Am Beautiful and Strong 75
Topic Cards 78

GLOSSARY 88

"Encouraging a child means that one or more of the following critical life messages are coming through, either by word or by action: I believe in you, I trust you, I know you can handle this, You are listened to, You are cared for, You are very important to me."

—BARBARA COLOROSO

INTRODUCTION

Dear Parents and Guardians,

The world around us seems to be changing and shifting at an ever-quickening pace. The consequence of this is that our young, innocent children are being exposed to adult problems and vices at younger and younger ages. But living in an ever-changing world also means that it is crucial that they develop their own intuitions about the world they are facing and that they learn to listen to their conscience to navigate difficult situations. As parents, we have a great opportunity and responsibility to teach our children how to find truth, how to value themselves, and how to love and respect others.

Joseph Fielding Smith taught, "The home … is the workshop where human characters are built and the manner in which they are formed depends upon the relationship existing between parents and the children. The home cannot be what it should be unless these relationships are of the proper character. Whether they are so or not depends, it is true, upon both parents and children, but much more upon parents. They must do their best."

This home "workshop" is the perfect place to have deep, purposeful conversations with your children, including talking about the power and sacredness of sexual intimacy. In this simple, yet powerful guide you have the tools you need to combat the unhealthy messages our young children are exposed to. By sharing your insight, knowledge, and experience about topics like love, healthy relationships, sexual intimacy, and outside dangers, you can prepare and protect your family from many of these destructive forces.

Our goal is to not only provide you with the essential information to start discussing these important topics, but we also hope you can create an environment in your home which encourages open conversations about many other issues which inevitably come up. By engaging in these discussions you will also be empowered to teach your children how to be safe, focus their curiosity, and prepare for future discussions and experiences.

WHAT'S INCLUDED

This curriculum includes 30 simple, yet meaningful lessons with helpful directions, and an extensive glossary of over 130 terms to assist you. Each lesson includes introductory points to consider, critical teaching information, powerful discussion questions, and additional resources to enrich your family's learning experience. Some topics even have an accompanying activity or song to inspire further conversation.

PREPARING FOR SUCCESS

- Consider your individual child's age, developmental stage, and personality in conjunction with each topic, as well as your family's values and individual situation. These will help you adapt the material in order to produce the best discussion. It's important that you begin your daily talks with just one topic in mind and that you make every experience, however brief, truly meaningful.

> *If you are positive and real with your child when it comes to talking about sexual intimacy, they will learn that you are available not just for this conversation, but for ANY discussion.*

If you feel that your child's knowledge is more advanced, please note that we have also developed this curriculum for other age groups and it is available for purchase. It's important to discuss things with your child based on their own maturity level, progressing or referring back at your own pace.

- Plan ahead of time, but don't create an event. Having a plan or planning ahead of time will remove much of the awkwardness you might feel in talking about these subjects with your child. In not creating an event, you are making the discussions feel more spontaneous, the experience more repeatable, and yourself more approachable.

- Please know, you do not need not be an expert to have meaningful, informative discussions with your kids. In fact, we feel strongly that leaning on your own personal experiences—both mistakes and successes—is a great way to use life lessons to teach your child. If done properly, these talks will bring you closer to your child than you could have ever imagined.

You know and love your child more than anyone, so you decide when and where these discussions take place. In time, you will recognize and enjoy teaching moments in everyday life with your child.

NEED TO KNOW

- This program is meant to be simple! It's organized into simple topics with bullet points that are straightforward and create conversations. Each lesson may only take 10 minutes, but make sure you allow more time for your child's questions and extra family discussion.

- This curriculum is not a one-discussion-fits-all. You guide the conversation and lead the discussion according to your unique situation. If you have three children, you will likely have three different conversations about the same topic.

- No program can cover all aspects of sexual intimacy perfectly for every individual circumstance. You can empower yourself with the knowledge you gain from this program to share with your child what you feel is the most important.

Please know, you do not need to be an expert to have meaningful, informative discussions with your child.

INSTRUCTIONS

ANSWER YOUR CHILD'S QUESTIONS

If you are embarrassed by your child's curiosity and questions, you're implying that there is something shameful about these topics. However, if you can answer those questions calmly and honestly, you're demonstrating that sexuality is positive, and that healthy relationships are something to look forward to when the time is right. Be sure to answer your child's questions practically and cheerfully and your child will learn that you are available not just for this discussion, but for any discussion. It's okay if you don't have all the answers, just tell them you will look for the answers and get back to them.

Create a Safe Zone

We recommend that you create a "safe zone" with your child and within your home. During the course of these conversations, your child should feel safe and free to ask any questions or make any comments without judgment or repercussions.

Your child should be able to use the term "safe zone" again and again to discuss, confide, and consult with you about the tough subjects they will be confronted with throughout life. It's highly recommended that, whenever possible, all parenting parties be involved in these discussions.

BE POSITIVE

Take the fear and shame out of these discussions. Sex is natural and wondrous, and your child should feel nothing but positivity about it from you. If you do feel awkward, stay calm and use matter-of-fact tones in your discussions. It's easier than you think—just open your mouth and begin! It will get easier with every talk you have. Even after just a few talks, both you and your child will begin to look forward to this time you are spending together. Use experiences from your own life to begin a discussion if it makes you feel more comfortable. We have listed some tough topics here, but they are all discussed in a positive, informative way. Don't worry, you've got this!

> Taking the time to talk about these topics will reiterate to your child how important they are to you.

FOCUS ON INTIMACY

Help your child understand how incredible and uniting sex can be. Don't just talk about the mechanics of sex. Spend a significant amount of time talking about the beauty of love and sex, the reality of human relationships, and how they are built and maintained. Children are constantly exposed to harmful examples of relationships in the media. Many of them are teaching your child lessons about sexuality and interactions between people that are misleading, incomplete, or purely unhealthy. Real emotional intimacy is rarely portrayed, so it's your job to teach and model what true intimacy actually is. Your child needs you to help connect the dots between healthy relationships and sexuality. Model positive ways for your child to care for, appreciate, protect, and develop a positive attitude about his or her body.

> You love and know your child better than anyone else, so you are the best person to judge what will be most effective.

BE THE SOURCE

Remember, you direct the conversations. Bring up the lesson points and questions that you feel are most important and allow the conversation to flow from there. You love and know your child better than anyone else, so you are the best person to judge what will be the most effective. Pause and take into account your personal values, beliefs, individual personalities, and family dynamics. You, the parent, can and should be the best source of information about sex and intimacy for your child. If you don't discuss these topics, your child will look for answers from other, less reliable and sometimes harmful sources on the internet, various media, or from other kids.

Finally, throughout these conversations, you'll want to keep up a continuous, nonjudgmental dialogue about the topics in order to foster a healthy, open relationship with your child. Begin your daily talks with just one topic in mind and endeavor to make every experience, however brief, truly meaningful.

Dina Alexander
Educate and Empower Kids

Let's Get Started!

Young children are not only innocent, but they are also naturally curious about their bodies and the world around them. This curriculum has been tailored to foster this curiosity. By bringing up points that lead towards open and honest conversations, these will facilitate ways to develop a healthy relationship with one's body.

It is also within these lessons that we hope you will plant the seeds of understanding healthy relationships, gender, boundaries and consent, and positive media choices. As you take time to discuss and explain the basics of anatomy, respect, relationships, pornography, etc., you will build and fortify your relationship with your child. By showing them that you care and are open to talking about body safety, respect, trust, and more, your child will learn that they can come to you for genuine, loving, and non-judgmental conversations.

1. Our Amazing Bodies

We get so used to living in our bodies that we often forget how special and amazing they really are. You may wish to direct this conversation in a way that helps your children see all of the incredible things their bodies can do. Bodies can run, jump, eat, feel, hug, swim, laugh, cry, etc. Emphasize that their bodies are unique. No one else in the whole world looks like or acts exactly like your child. No one else runs precisely like them or smiles just like them.

Help your child to understand that they experience the world through their body. Take time to discuss their five senses: hearing, seeing, tasting, touching, smelling.

Start the Conversation
Introduce the topic by having your child touch a book, an ice cube, or their favorite stuffed animal. Prompt them to describe what they feel (hard, cold, soft, etc.) Ask them how they would touch things if they didn't have their hands or skin to feel with. Help them realize that their body teaches them about the world around them.

Talk about things we can do when we are holding still or have a disability that may inhibit things such as thinking, seeing, talking, listening, learning, counting, reading, smiling, understanding, and more. Remind them that each person sees, feels, smells, tastes, and hears the world differently.

Questions for Your Child
- What can you hear, see, smell, taste, and feel?
- What are some powerful things your body can do?
- Why do we need our bodies?

- What are some things we can do to take care of the outside of our bodies?
- What are some things we can do to take care of the inside of our bodies?

Activity

Do one or more of the following activities that explore our senses. If you feel that it may enhance the experience, ask your child if they would like to experience some of these blindfolded.

Tasting: Have your child taste a variety of herbs or foods such as salt, lemon, honey, celery, etc.

Smelling: Have your child smell a variety of items such as laundry detergent, perfume, flowers, dinner cooking, coffee, cinnamon, etc.

Hearing: Play a variety of sounds or go on a "sound drive" to experience different sounds such as traffic flowing, horns honking, trains passing, people talking, music playing, a person singing, a baby crying, wind blowing, etc.

Touching: Give your child various items to touch such as sandpaper, leaves, a hairbrush, warm water, a soft cloth, etc.

Seeing: Show your child a video or photos of people and places around the world. Talk about the beautiful variety of people and landscapes found throughout.

As they experience each variety, encourage them to slow down and truly experience what they are hearing, seeing, tasting, smelling, or feeling. Discuss how some sights, sounds, and smells are welcoming and comforting. Talk about those that warn us, such as smoke or gasoline. Remind your child that some experiences affect multiple senses at the same time such as holding and eating a warm cookie, or walking outside in the rain.

Additional Resources:

"Positive Body Image Starts with Mom" from Educate and Empower Kids
A great article that reminds us our kids are watching and listening to us. If we want our kids to value their bodies, we need to set an example for them.

"An Hour of Play Every Day: 77 Things to do Outside!" from Educate and Empower Kids
This article talks about the benefits of playing outside with your kids, but also lists a lot of great ideas for what to do while you're out there.

"Teach Your Child Body Gratitude" from Educate and Empower Kids
This article goes through a few different ways to teach children how great their bodies are, and how they can show gratitude for them.

"Teaching Kids About Healthy Body Image: Tips from the Experts at Beauty Redefined" from the Educate and Empower Kids
Body Image experts Lindsay and Lexie Kite share their most valuable insights in teaching our kids how to appreciate their amazing bodies.

2.
My Body Belongs To Me

A child who understands that their body belongs to them and no one else is far more empowered to say "no" or get away from a person who makes them uncomfortable. There is far more

danger to a child who has been taught to acquiesce to an adult or peer who wants to hug or kiss them without regard for their feelings or instincts.

Start the Conversation
Explain to your child that because they are unique and special, they are valuable. Help them understand that we take care of things that we value (for example, how do they treat a favorite toy or another special item in your home?). Teach them that other people may not understand or respect a person's value, so they need to learn to stand up for themselves and their boundaries. Tell your child that it is normal to share toys, but we do not share our bodies.

An additional topic that may be covered here is that of forced affection: how do you handle it in your family when someone, such as an aunt or uncle, demands a kiss or hug from your child? If necessary, create a plan for what your child can do if they are uncomfortable with a friend's, family member, or other person's affection.

 FORCED AFFECTION: *Pressuring or forcing a child to give a hug, kiss, or any other form of physical affection when they do not have the desire to do so.*

Questions for Your Child

- What makes you special?
- What should you do if someone wants to give you a hug and you don't want to?
- What are some things that make you special and valuable?
- What should you do when someone wants to give you a hug or kiss when you don't want to?
- Why does your body belong to you and no one else?
- What is a boundary? (see the glossary for definition)

Activity

Give your child some chalk and in the driveway or on the sidewalk, have them draw a circle around themself. Let them make it in whatever shape they want. Then explain how that circle is like a boundary they can make for themself. Boundaries are rules we can set to protect ourselves and ensure that we will feel comfortable and happy with others.

> "A child must know that he is a miracle, that since the beginning of the world there hasn't been, and until the end of the world there will not be, another child like him."
>
> -PABLO CASALS

Additional Resources:

"Sexual Assault Awareness - Conversation Starters to Protect Your Children" from Educate and Empower Kids
This article provides parents with some foundational information regarding the frequency of sexual assault, and what they can do to help teach their children how to protect themselves.

"Kids and 'Affection': Why I'm NOT Teaching My Kids To Be Polite" from Educate and Empower Kids
This article talks about teaching kids to speak up when they feel uncomfortable with unwanted affection.

"Lesson: Teaching Your Kids Healthy Boundaries" from Educate and Empower Kids
This family night lesson was created to help teach kids the importance of boundaries and how they can trust their instincts to keep those boundaries from being crossed.

"Helping Children Develop Healthy Sexual Attitudes" from Educate and Empower Kids
Understanding the power of arousal templates and creating open dialogues in your home will help your child to not only develop healthy sexual attitudes, but build a satisfying sex life based in intimacy and connection.

3. Male Anatomy

Our bodies are very special, and we are each unique in our own ways. It's so important for our kids to understand what their bodies are and how they work. Spend time discussing the differences and similarities of males and females. Use the glossary to help you discuss male anatomy (penis, testicles/scrotum, anus) with your child. If you only have a male child, it is still very important to teach the following lesson on female anatomy.

If possible, discuss with your spouse how you would like to approach this topic with your children. Share the responsibility of teaching these topics with your spouse. Take time to think and plan this lesson if you are unsure how to start the conversation.

Start the Conversation

Help your child to understand the unique body parts that boys have. Children may have questions concerning the way a penis can change during an erection. It is completely normal for infants, toddlers, and boys to experience erections for a variety of reasons. They may also have questions regarding what a penis is "for" (at this age, primarily urination).

If your child has questions, answer them clearly and avoid associating shame or embarrassment with this natural bodily function. Help them understand that a penis

 PENIS: *The external, male sexual organ comprised of the shaft, foreskin, glans penis, and meatus. The penis contains the urethra, through which both urine and semen travel to exit the body.*

is personal and private. If you feel your child is ready, help them understand that, in the future, the function of the penis goes beyond urination.

Questions for your Child

- Why do we need males and females on Earth?
- Are you male or female?
- What body parts do you have that are different from girls?
- Sometimes people use other words for the word penis. Why should we use the word "penis"?
- Do you understand how your penis works?
- Why are your bottom and penis private parts of your body? How should we treat our private parts?
- What can we do to keep every part of our body safe?

Sample Dialogue

Parent: Sometimes people use other funny words to describe body parts like the penis. Why is it helpful to use the word "penis"? *(Allow your child to answer.)*

Parent: It's important to use real words instead of funny words so that we don't get confused or confuse other people.

> Help your son understand that he is a strong and unique individual who is loved because of who he is!

Additional Resources:

"Introducing Children to Anatomy" from the National Library of Medicine
This article talks about the benefits of children learning about their own anatomy, specifically through fun activities, and how it may make way for a healthier society.

"Lesson: Teaching Healthy Body Image to Boys" from Educate and Empower Kids
Knowing anatomically correct terms for bodies is so important to starting kids out with healthy body image. This lesson talks about how to continue teaching your boys how to have a healthy body image.

"Building A Better Body Image: 4 Ways to Boost Yours and Your Kids' Self-Worth" from Educate and Empower Kids
This article goes through a few ways to help you think better about yourself so that you will have the ability to boost your child's self-worth as well.

"20 Ways to Compliment A Child That Have Nothing To Do With Appearance" from Educate and Empower Kids
There are a lot of good things about our kids and we want them to know that! This article can help you show your kids what you love most about them.

4. Female Anatomy

Every part of our body is beautiful and special. Take time to explain the amazing and important differences between boys and girls. Sex organs, or our "private parts," are the most basic way that girls are different from boys. Explain that a doctor can look at a baby and know the sex of a baby.

When discussing both male and female anatomy, it is important to remember to use correct terminology when referring to each body part. Your child should not be embarrassed or ashamed of any part of his or her body. It is also important to remind children that we talk about genitals privately because they are special and personal.

Use the glossary to help you discuss female anatomy (vagina, urethra, anus, breasts/nipples, vulva). If you only have a female child, it is still very important to teach the previous lesson on male anatomy. Just as your daughter will be curious about herself, she will also be curious about others. Teaching our children about the opposite sex not only allows you to direct the conversation in a healthy, accurate manner, it also helps your children to develop respect and understanding of the opposite sex.

If possible, we also suggest that you share the responsibility of teaching with your partner or spouse.

VULVA: *The parts of the female sexual organs that are on the outside of the body.*

VAGINA: *The muscular tube leading from the external genitals to the cervix of the uterus in women. During sexual intercourse, the penis can be inserted into the vagina. During childbirth, the infant exits the uterus through the vagina.*

Start the Conversation

Help your child to understand the unique body parts that girls have. If they have questions about these body parts, answer the question simply, define terminology, and do not get distracted by additional unnecessary details such as the mechanics of intercourse or birth. See glossary for definitions of vagina, urethra, anus, and nipples/breast.

Questions for Your Child

- Why do we have both males and females on our planet? Are you male or female?
- What body parts do you have that are different from boys?
- Do you understand why you have a vagina AND a urethra?
- Do you understand what your anus is for?
- Sometimes people use other words for the word vagina. Why is it helpful or important to use the word "vagina"?

Sample Dialogue

Parent: Sometimes people use other funny words to describe body parts like the vagina or breasts. Why is it helpful to use the word "vagina" or "breasts"? *(Allow your child to answer.)*

Parent: It's important to use real words instead of funny words so that we don't get confused or confuse other people.

Additional Resources:

"'The Talk(s)': Start Off Easy" from Educate and Empower Kids
This article takes the reader through a few ways to ease into these crucial but sometimes difficult talks, such as curiosity, appropriate touch, and pornography.

"Inspiring Kids to Choose Their Own Body Image" from Educate and Empower Kids
Knowledge about anatomically correct words helps kids be aware of their bodies and promotes a healthy body image. This article goes through a few more ways to teach kids about body image.

"Positive Body Image Starts With Moms" from Educate and Empower Kids
More often than not, kids look to their moms for how to behave and treat themselves and others, so it's crucial for moms to show them a positive body image from the start, which can be hard.

"The Powerful Role Dads Plays in a Child's Life" from Educate and Empower Kids
Just as mothers play a vital role in their children's lives, father's play an equally powerful role in their sons and daughters' lives–that no one else can truly fill.

5. Respecting Others

Each child has value, and everyone has boundaries. These boundaries are different for each person. Help your child understand that even if they don't like someone's boundaries, they still need to respect them. Discuss "personal space." Use the glossary to explain what a boundary is. Have your kids show you where their own personal space bubble is.

some people enjoy lots of physical contact, while for other people it can be uncomfortable and overwhelming. Let your child know that they can ask people about their boundaries. The goal during this discussion is to educate your child so that they know they can learn how to engage with others socially and how to ask about other's boundaries.

Start the Conversation
Ask your child what it means for someone to have value. Discuss the value and specialness of the people they love most. As you discuss the concept of boundaries, explain that

Questions for Your Child
- What does it mean to show respect to someone?
- How can you show respect and kindness to others? (Parents, teachers, friends, siblings, etc.)
- How can you show respect and kindness to yourself?
- How should other people treat you? How should you treat others?
- How would you ask an adult about their boundaries? Is it ever appropriate to ask adults about their boundaries?
- How would you ask a friend about his/her boundaries? When should you ask friends about their boundaries?

Sample Dialogue
(for child to practice)

    Child: Can I give you a hug?

    Child: Can I hold your hand to cross the street?

Discuss appropriate responses to these questions if a friend, teacher, relative, or stranger asks these questions. Talk about why it's important to ask first before doing anything like hugging or kissing or tickling, etc. Talk with your child about how they would like to be treated, and ask if they think they should treat others that way too.

Activity

Write down the following statements on small slips of paper. Have each person in your family take a slip of paper. If you have a small family, feel free to let each person take more than one, then have each person take a turn saying what is on their slip of paper (or read it out loud for your younger children). Discuss whether or not the behavior on the slip of paper is showing respect. Ask your children what they would do in each situation.

- Helping a friend clean up the toys you both played with
- Yelling at your brother when they accidentally break your toy
- Giving a hug to your sister who is sad
- Running away when your mom calls for you to come home
- Telling someone in your class that you don't like their clothes
- Inviting a new person in your class to play with you
- Not cleaning up your dog's poop after he goes on your neighbor's lawn
- Telling your grandma that you love her

Additional Resources:

"Teaching Your Children Self-Respect and Respect for Others" from Educate and Empower Kids
Something children must be taught is how to respect another person, and this can be a difficult lesson to teach. This article gives some insight on how to go about this.

"Kids in the Digital Age: The Challenge of Expressing Emotions Healthily" from Educate and Empower Kids
It's so important for kids to learn how to treat themselves and others with kindness. This article has some great tips on how to start teaching kindness and emotional regulation.

"Sibling Rivalry: The Good, bad, and the In-between" from Educate and Empower Kids
For those of you who have multiple children, here is an article about how to deal with sibling squabbling and everything that goes on with that. This will help you teach your kids that their feelings affect one another and themselves.

"Creating Rules and Boundaries with Your Family" from Educate and Empower Kids
This article includes a variety of tips and tricks that parents can use when setting boundaries for their children.

6. Public

Hold a family night meeting about "public vs. private" things and what is appropriate to do in both. Feel free to combine this lesson with the following lesson, #7, "Private." This is a great opportunity to discuss how keeping certain information private can keep us safe.

What does the word "public" mean? What are some things we do in public? What are some things we do not do in public? Help your child understand the fundamental difference between public and private.

> The internet is public. When we are online, it is like being in public. We need to be careful online: where we go, what games we play, and who we talk to.

Use the glossary and sample dialogue below to teach your child what the word public means.

> **Note:** *Parents, please make sure your child is physically and mentally capable of understanding these rules before they are implemented.*

Start the Conversation

It's important for your child to understand the difference between public and private. These can be difficult concepts for young children, as they may not have experience with this yet. Discuss the different types of things that one does in public while mentioning some of your family's favorite public places such as the park, church, stores, the neighborhood, etc. Focus your discussion on what we do with our bodies and what we do with our words in public places.

To help your child grasp the concept, link "public" and "private" with concrete locations and specific behaviors. As an example, we have provided a sample dialogue, located on the next column, to illustrate how this can be done. Along with this, it is vital for your child to learn how the concept of private and public functions online with games, websites, and apps–more on this in the next lesson.

Questions for Your Child

- What does the word "public" mean?
- What are some things we do in public?
- What are some things we do not do in public?
- Where are the public places we can go?
- What might happen if we talk about private things while we are in public?

Sample Dialogue

Parent: "Public" means something that everyone can do, a place where everyone can be, or something that everyone can see.

We are in public when we go to the library, the park, or to school. When we are in public, we can talk, laugh, play, read, eat, walk, etc.

We do not remove our clothing in public. We do not urinate in public. We do not touch our bodies where our underwear covers us in public.

> "You don't know how much you appreciate your privacy until you don't have it."
>
> —MORGAN FREEMAN

Additional Resources:

"Talking to Kids About Public vs. Private Discussions" from Educate and Empower Kids
"Children are public creatures. They are not born with a sense of what should be discussed in private and what should not."

"Talking To Your Child About Their Body and Private Parts" from Children's MD
This article talks about how to discuss these kinds of topics with children, and what behaviors to expect and certain ages.

7. Private

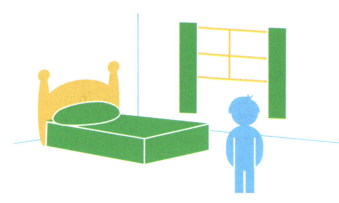

Help your kids understand that private things refer to our bodies or topics related to sexuality, and also information regarding us personally, where we live, private family information, etc. Take the time to discuss why this kind of information is private. This is a great time to talk about the difference between a secret and keeping certain information private.

Start the Conversation
Begin by discussing various behaviors we do in private. In private, we get dressed, we use the bathroom, we clean ourselves, and many other things.

Talk about certain thoughts and comments that we can keep to ourselves, as well as when it's appropriate to share personal experiences and stories. It is also important for your child to understand how the concepts of private and public function online since much of our children's lives exist online. Ask your child what are some things that are okay to say online (public)? What are some things we should NOT share online? Then, explain some of the things that we don't share online with strangers, including our name, phone number, school name, and home address.

> Children are public creatures. They are not born with a sense of what should be discussed in private and what should not. Instead, they are more concerned with taking pride in understanding how their bodies work and all of the new words they have learned.

Questions for Your Child

- What does "private" mean? What are some things we do in private?
- Where are private places we can go?
- What is a secret?
- What are some thoughts we have that we should keep to ourselves?
- Some things we only talk about in private. Some things we can talk about in public (a TV show, a favorite toy, the weather, etc.). Every family has its own rules about this. What are some things that we DON'T talk about in public?
- Once we are old enough and capable of going to the bathroom on our own, why is it important to use the bathroom alone?

Sample Dialogue

Parent: "Private" means something that is just for you, or for some things just for you and your family. We can take baths in private. We go to the bathroom in private. We can be naked in private. Our bedrooms can be private. Our bathrooms can be private.

> **Developmental Note:** *In order to develop a healthy attitude towards privacy and self-sufficiency, it is important to help children understand that they need to go to the bathroom by themselves as soon as they are physically capable of doing so. This does not mean that parents should rush their child to be toilet trained, but rather that after a child is toilet trained (at the point they are ready for it), they should be encouraged to use the bathroom without their friends or others present. An exception should be made for those who need physical assistance to successfully use a bathroom.*

Additional Resources:

"From Awkward to Awesome: Talking to Your Kids about Sexual Intimacy" from Educate and Empower Kids
This video discusses several strategies of how to talk about sexual intimacy with your kids, and how you can make it feel natural instead of awkward.

"Lesson: Think Before You Speak, Post or Hit Send" from Educate and Empower Kids
This lesson was made to help teach kids the ripples that they can make by saying or posting something thoughtlessly.

"Do You Know Where Your Kids Are Online?" from Educate and Empower Kids
"The internet is an amazing place. Similar to a big, metropolitan city, there is so much to explore. In big cities like New York, there are museums, parks, concerts, Broadway, restaurants, and sites to see, but there are also areas to avoid.

8. Clothing

Help your child understand the term "appropriate" in terms of an item fitting or working in a specific context. Different events have different purposes and can require different clothing choices. For example, we wear swimsuits at the beach so we can get wet. It would not be appropriate to wear a swimsuit in the middle of a winter snowstorm because we would get cold and possibly sick.

Start the Conversation
Tell your child that they are loved and worth protecting. That's why you're having this conversation. Then teach them how to run through the following checklist when picking out clothes:

WHO is wearing and seeing the clothes?

WHERE will the clothes be worn?

WHY are the clothes being worn?

WHAT are the positives and negatives about the clothes being worn?

HOW well will these clothes work to meet my needs?

Remind them of the lesson about how our bodies are amazing, and that we dress appropriately to be comfortable and to show care and respect to ourselves.

Questions for Your Child
- How do clothes protect us?
- What does a firefighter wear? What does an astronaut or a ballerina wear?
- How do clothes help people do their jobs?
- How do we protect our bodies by wearing clothes?

- Q What clothing do we feel is appropriate for people in our family to wear?
- Q What do we wear in winter? What do we wear to the beach? To school?
- Q Why can't we just go to the mall or attend school naked?
- Q What does being modest mean to you?
- Q How do you feel when you are in public, dressed comfortably and modestly?

Activity
Have a variety of dress up options available, like scarves, sweaters, sun hats, shoes, sandals, etc. You could even include dress up outfits of different occupations like firefighters or astronauts. Then have your child play charades with the clothes where they pick an item and then you guess what they are or what activity they're doing. Afterward, discuss why certain clothing is worn for certain places, and what is appropriate in some places may not be in others. Ask your child to explain how clothes can protect our bodies.

> A smart clothing choice is one that "investigates" the context where the clothes will be worn, and asks Who, Where, Why, What, and How. When our kids understand how to be smart about their clothes, they can choose clothing that is functional, comfortable, attractive, and even an expression of their personal style.

Additional Resources:

"Modesty and Smart Clothing Choices: Teaching Our Kids to Be Seen for Who They Are" from Educate and Empower Kids
"A smart clothing choice is one that 'investigates' the context where the clothes will be worn, and asks Who, Where, Why, What, and How. When our kids understand how to be smart about their clothes, they can choose clothing that is functional, comfortable, attractive, and even an expression of their personal style."

"Teaching our Kids Smart Clothing Choices and Modesty" from Educate and Empower Kids
The purpose of this family night lesson is to make sure your child understands how to make clothing choices that are appropriate for different occasions and to help them learn to respect their body and protect themselves.

9. Good Touch

One way we show people we care about them is through touch. Even animals show affection through various forms of touch. Talk with your child about the various ways your family shows affection to each other. Ask your child if they have seen other families at school or in their community show affection in other ways.

This lesson may be more effective if done in conjunction with the following lesson, "Bad Touch".

Be positive: Your number one job is to empower your child so they have positive feelings about their bodies and feel safe in the knowledge that they have someone to talk to if there is a problem.

Start the Conversation

Explain to your child the many positive ways you can show affection: hugs, kisses, backrubs, holding hands, saying "I love you," etc. Discuss the ways your family shows physical affection, and discuss what is appropriate and what is not. Take time to learn how your child likes to receive affection. Touch? Words? Time together? Someone doing something nice for them?

Talk about how powerful and significant human touch can be. It can calm, soothe, anger, or hurt people. Touch can be used to express love or frustration.

Questions for Your Child

- Can you think of ways that people or even animals express affection to each other?
- What kind of touch do you like best? Kisses? High fives?
- What are some ways that our family shows affection?
- Do you like hugs and spending time together? Do you like to hear "I love you"?
- Do you like to sit on someone's lap? Do you like playing together?
- Out of all the ways our family shows love, which ones are your favorites?

Activity
Have your child list some of their favorite types of touch. These could be hugs, kisses, high fives, pats on the shoulder, holding hands, fist bumps, etc. Let them act out each one with you. Ask them why those are their favorites and how it makes them feel. Ask if they prefer to give a hug, kiss, etc. or to receive affection. Share with them your favorites and talk about how it makes you feel. Discuss how it feels good when you share this kind of affection from people you love.

> **Help your children understand what safe and appropriate touch is. Good touch is something that will give a safe and happy feeling. Parents' touches are usually comforting and pleasant.**

Additional Resources:

"A Family Night Lesson About Good Touch/Bad Touch" from Educate and Empower Kids
It's crucial to teach your kids how to recognize good touch from bad touch. Teach in a way that builds trust between you and your kids, that will allow them to come to you.

"How Teaching Healthy Sexuality Can Help Your Child Against the Predator, the Pressuring Partner, and the Prude" from Educate and Empower Kids
In their future relationships, it's crucial for kids to know how to protect themselves from a person who might pressure them into anything they are uncomfortable with.

"My Body is Mine: Teaching Kids Appropriate Touch" from Educate and Empower Kids
This article gives some helpful suggestions on how to start the conversation with your child about what is a good touch and what is not.

"Lesson: Kindness: Online, Face to Face, and Everywhere" from Educate and Empower Kids
This lesson is a great help in guiding you through teaching your little ones how to learn those basics.

10. Bad Touch

As you teach this concept to your child, you must be specific and clear. As you discuss inappropriate touch, ask your child if they understand and have them repeat back to you what they have heard from you.

Sometimes a child may think that they will be punished if they tell an adult about a "bad" experience that happened to them simply because they were there during the experience. Help your child to understand that they are not in trouble if someone touches them where their underwear covers or in a way that makes them feel uncomfortable or confused.

> *Although we are using the more universal term "bad touch," please teach your child that if someone touches them where their bathing suit covers them that they, the child, is NOT bad.*

Check out our helpful article "8 Ways a Predator Might Groom Your Child" and discuss common grooming techniques with your child.

Start the Conversation

Explain to your child that sometimes a friend or grown-up may touch them in a way that makes them feel uncomfortable, sad, angry, or just plain icky. Specifically mention their anatomy that no one should touch: penis, scrotum, anus, vulva, vagina, nipples, bottom, etc.

TEST TOUCH: *Seemingly innocent touches by a predator or offender, such as a pat on the back or a squeeze on the arm, that are meant to normalize kids to being in physical contact with the predator. Test touches can quickly progress from these innocent touches to more dangerous and damaging ones.*

To help them remember, keep it simple and use the general rule of thumb that no one should touch them where their bathing suit covers, except a doctor, and only if Mom or Dad is present.

Teach your child that if they report something like this happening that they are NOT in trouble and that you will believe your child. Most small children have trouble articulating where they were touched or if they were even touched inappropriately. This is why it is so important to teach our kids correct anatomy terms. As parents you need to trust your instincts if you feel uncomfortable with an adult or teen in your child's life.

Questions for Your Child

- What is a "bad touch"? What makes it wrong?
- If a grown up touches you where your bathing suit covers, is this your fault? (No! Grown-ups know they should NOT touch you where your bathing suit covers your body.)
- What should you do if a grown-up or older child touches you in a way that makes you feel uncomfortable? How can you get away from that person?
- Is it ok for a _____ [teacher, coach, babysitter, etc.] to stroke your hair?

For young children, keep it simple. Give them simple rules:

1. Nobody should be hurting you.
2. Nobody should be touching your private parts.
3. Nobody should take photos of your private parts.
4. Don't keep secrets if someone is hurting you.
5. If you have a problem, tell somebody.
6. Tell someone if you are being bullied.

- What kind of hug is ok with your teacher? With people from church? With your friends?
- Can bad touch happen even when you have clothes on?

Sample Dialogue

Parent: What should you do if someone touches you in a way that makes you feel uncomfortable?

Child: I don't know.

Parent: If anyone touches you where your underwear covers or in a way that makes you feel uncomfortable or confused, tell me or _____ (name an adult you trust).

Child: Mom, someone helped me go to the bathroom and it made me uncomfortable.

Parent: Please tell me what happened. Remember, you are safe with me and loved.

Child: Dad, someone helped me tuck in my shirt and I didn't like it.

Parent: Thank you for telling me. Let's talk about what happened so I can understand it better and help you.

Additional Resources:

"The Secret I Almost Did Not Tell" from Educate and Empower Kids
This article talks of the personal experience a woman had with inappropriate touch as a child, and how she used that experience to learn how to protect her own child in the present.

"Child Predators: What Every Parent Should Know" from Educate and Empower Kids
This video goes over a few tools that predators use, and how we as parents can counter these with knowledge.

"Helping Your Child Become the Master of Their Body Moving Beyond Good Touch/Bad Touch" from Educate and Empower Kids
This family night lesson was put together to help you navigate teaching your child about the different kinds of touches, and what to do if they experience a "bad touch," and how to avoid it as well.

11. Predators

Many parents worry about starting a discussion about predators with their kids because they think they are stealing their child's innocence. However, you are not scaring them, you are empowering them with knowledge. By discussing dangers, you are not only giving your children the information needed to avoid predators, but you are also giving your kids the words to communicate with you if someone is acting strangely or hurting them.

While it may be hard to understand, it's important that your children know that predators can be friends, neighbors, or even family members. Help them feel comfortable enough to come to you about it, even if the predator is someone close.

> **Note:** *This is a lesson that needs to be repeated a few times so that your child can fully understand your words, have time to process the topic, and to ask questions later.*

(SEXUAL) PREDATOR: *A sexual predator is someone who seeks to obtain sexual contact/pleasure from another through predatory and/or abusive behavior. The term is often used to describe the deceptive and coercive methods used by people who commit sex crimes where there is a victim.*

Start the Conversation

As you begin this discussion, avoid blanket assumptions (such as, "We trust our teachers") because, unfortunately, that is not always true. Also explain that just because you "know" someone does not automatically mean that they are a trusted adult. Be specific and concrete in your planning in order to reassure and empower your child.

Discuss the fact that most people in the world are good, and mention some people you know in your family and community who are good, upright individuals. Explain to your child that there are some bad people in the world. Use stories and current events to discuss certain people who are bad. With your child, make a list of people you trust. This should be a very short list of people you absolutely trust with your child's life.

Create a plan that your children can put into action if they are in a scary situation.

Consider employing a code word or "safe word" (a secret word that you agree on as a family) that you can give to other adults to let your child know that it is ok to do what that adult says.

For example, if another adult needs to pick them up from school in the case of an emergency. A safe word can also be used when your child calls you and wants to be picked up immediately to get out of certain, uncomfortable situations (when pornography is present, when someone has touched them inappropriately, etc.). This can be the same word or a different word entirely.

Questions for Your Child

- Who are the people that you ARE comfortable with? Why?
- Is there anyone that you get an "icky" feeling around?
- Who are some adults we trust?
- What can you do if an adult makes you uncomfortable?
- What can you do if an older child or adult wants to be alone with you, or they try to touch you when you don't want them to?
- Who is someone at school/church/soccer/etc. that you can talk to if Mom or Dad is not there?

Your child needs to know if abuse occurs that :

- They are not to blame and should not feel guilty.

- It is important to tell a trusted adult so that the abuse can stop.

- The person that has abused them needs to get help for their problem so that they will stop hurting children. And that is why it is so important to tell.

- What do you do if someone tries to get you to keep a secret from your parents?
- What do you do if someone is giving you special attention or treats that they aren't giving to your friends or siblings?
- What should you do if a friend tells you someone has touched them in a way that made them uncomfortable or hurt them?
- What is a code word we can have/use so that you know if a person is someone your parents trust?

Note: *Remind your child that a person must give the child the code word if they are picking your child up from school or sports. If the code is not given then the child is to run away and find a trusted adult.*

Activity

Practice using your family code word with your children. Let them know that only people your family trusts will have the code word. Roleplay a couple different scenarios like someone picking them up from school.

> **Parent:** Do you go with the person if they say_____? (Not the code word)
>
> **Child:** No!
>
> **Parent:** Do you go with the person if they say_____? (The code word)
>
> **Child:** Yes!

Additional Resources:

"What Online Predators Don't Want YOU to Do" from Educate and Empower Kids
This article goes through what to be aware of with online dangers that would draw kids into the reach of predators, then gives parents some good tips on how to deal with those dangers.

"Can You Spot the Grooming Behaviors of a Predator?" from Educate and Empower Kids
This page goes through some of the common practices known as "grooming," and how to look out for those and how they could be used on your child.

"A Lesson for Teaching Your Children About Predators" from Educate and Empower Kids
In this family night lesson, we outline how to proceed with a conversation to teach your kids about predators and what they can look for, as well as establishing trust between you so that they will feel comfortable coming to you if anything happens.

12. How To Say "No"

Learning to say "no!" to an adult may not seem like a skill that you want to teach your child, or one that they might already seem to know. However, there's a big difference between a child saying "no" to a parent about cleaning up their toys and saying "no" to an adult who is trying to manipulate and hurt them. It's an important skill that needs to be developed and practiced.

It's also important for every family to discuss who are the trusted adults in your child's life. If there are known issues with any adults with whom your child has contact (including family members), create an appropriate plan with your child to deal with the situation. This may include things like not being alone with the person, not going places (especially alone) with the person, staying in your home's open area or yard, and not going into a bedroom with the person, or for a ride in someone's car, etc.

Note: *This is a lesson that will need to be repeated several times.*

Start the Conversation

Many times children find it hard to say "no" to others. They do not want to disappoint a loved one or authority figure, or to be left out or rejected. It is important that you help your child understand that saying "no" is okay and necessary sometimes. Even if they do not completely understand or respond right away to this lesson, it is still crucial to plant this seed of knowledge and empowerment in their hearts and minds.

Practice saying "no" firmly and then practice yelling "no!"

Questions for Your Child

- You can say "no" to anyone. When is it okay to say "no"?
- Was there ever a time that you had to say "no"? What happened?
- Is there a time when it's okay to say "no" to your parents?
- Does saying "no" make you a bad person? (No! You can always say "no" and still be a very good person.)

Activity

Help your child to understand when it's ok to say no to an adult by giving them specific examples:

OK to say no:
- When someone asks to see your private parts.
- When someone tries to show you pornography.
- When someone tries to give you a hug and you don't want to.

NOT ok to say no:
- When Mom or Dad tells you to pick up your toys.

Remind your child that even though they have told an adult or older child "no," they can and should still tell you about the situation. Guide your child through various scenarios where they might have to say "no" and how they should handle it.

Additional Resources:

"How to Identify A Child Predator Online" from Educate and Empower Kids
This article lists a series of terms, code words, and symbols that predators use to secretly identify themselves with other predators, and goes through what each means.

"Your Child Needs to Know: What is a Predator?" from Educate and Empower Kids
"Before we can prepare our children to know how to recognize a predator, we must first be clear on what classifies someone as such. Here are some facts to keep at the forefront of our minds while keeping our children out of danger."

13. Your Instincts Keep You Safe

As you prepare to discuss instincts with your child, keep in mind your child's individual level of maturity and development. Teach them that no matter what, if someone else decides to hurt them, that is the perpetrator's fault and NOT your child's.

Remember, the goal of this conversation is not to create fear, but rather to help your child recognize the feelings they might have in response to dangers, be it bullying or predatory behavior. Consider doing the helpful activity within this lesson, then afterward go through the questions section together with your child.

Start the Conversation
In order to explain the term "instinct" to your child, consider using the following simplified definition: something you know without learning it or thinking about it. Teach them that those instincts are there to let you know when something feels bad or "icky."

Questions for Your Child
- What are instincts? What do instincts feel like?
- What does that "icky" feeling mean?
- Have you ever had that "icky" or "scary" feeling?
- What should we do when we think or feel something is bad or not safe?

INSTINCTS: *An inherent response or inclination toward a particular behavior. An action or reaction that is performed without being based on prior experience.*

Explain to them that some instincts can keep us safe by warning us that something might be dangerous to their body or mind. Empower your child by helping them to recognize helpful, instinctive responses. Along with this, share a story from your life with your child about when you felt like you needed to do something. Did you listen or not? What was the consequence of that action?

Activity
To help your child understand the role instincts can play, consider asking them how they feel when they:
- See an animal or insect they are afraid of
- See their favorite food
- Hear the bell to go outside to recess
- Hear a siren from a firetruck or police car

> Protect your kids by preparing them. By teaching them about the wonder and beauty of their bodies and minds. By warning them that there are those who would corrupt and hurt them if they got the chance.

Additional Resources:

"Why the Best Way to Protect Our Children is to Prepare Them" from Educate and Empower Kids
This article talks of why there's so much need to prepare and empower your children with knowledge that will protect them. We as parents can't always be with them, so we must prepare them to protect themselves.

"For Parents: How to Have A Family Council" from Educate and Empower Kids
This page teaches how to effectively have a family council. This is the perfect place to teach your kids how to trust in that gut feeling they may have when something doesn't feel right.

14. You Have Feelings & Emotions That Connect You

Defining emotions can sometimes be challenging. Use your family experiences to help you more concretely explain feelings and emotions to your child. The animated film "Inside Out" can also be helpful in explaining these abstract concepts.

The point of this topic is to focus on the good and positive things that come out of family relationships. The healthy interactions that show love and concern should be stressed here.

Start the Conversation

Explain to your child that there are many different kinds of feelings between all people; friends and family, and people we know at school or church, etc. These can be both positive and negative. Help your child to understand what those feelings could be and what they can do with them.

Go through some of the positive and negative feelings your child might have for the people around them (happiness and excitement with friends, love and warmth with family, and anger, hurt, or frustration when they're having a hard time with someone). Discuss how these feelings can come about and why. As an example, talk about how your love for your child grew. Feel free to share an experience from your own life when you had negative feelings for someone and how you handled that.

Explain that positive and negative feelings connect us to other people. Often, our feelings affect other people

 EMOTION: *An emotion is a feeling such as happiness, love, fear, sadness, or anger, which can be caused by the situation that you are in or the people you are with.*

and their feelings can affect us as well. Give your child an example of this. Then, let your child talk about how other people's emotions have affected them. Discuss the feelings you have for your child and spouse. Ask your child to share some of their feelings for friends, grandparents, neighbors, and even strangers–noting that they may not have any feelings toward strangers. Talk about how we have different feelings with different people and in different situations.

Questions for Your Child

- Everyone has feelings. When do you feel happy? When do you feel sad?
- What other feelings can we have? Why do we have feelings?
- Feelings help us to know when we love and care about someone. When you do something nice for your mom, how do you feel?
- Think about your friends: how do you feel about them? How do they feel about you?
- What kinds of feelings make you happy?
- When someone does something nice for you, how do you feel?
- How can you express your emotions in a healthy way?

Activity

Practice helping your child identify feelings. Present a few positive and negative scenarios to your child and ask them how it makes them feel. Then work through that feeling with them and how they can deal with it in a healthy way.

Parent: Someone took a toy from you at the playground. How does that make you feel?

Child: It makes me mad.

Parent: It's okay to feel mad. First let's take a few breaths and calm down. What would you do next?

Child: Ask for my toy back.

Parent: And if they don't give it back?

Child: Ask for help.

Additional Resources:

"Emotional Intelligence is Critical to Creating Strong Kids" from Educate and Empower Kids
This article discusses the importance of teaching children the value of emotional intelligence.

"Empower Your Child Today Through Positive Self-Talk and Affirmations" from Educate and Empower Kids
This article goes through various ways to boost self-confidence and healthy feelings in your child.

"Emotional Intelligence: An Essential Skill in Our Kids' Tech Saturated World" from Educate and Empower Kids
This article talks about the importance of teaching our kids emotional intelligence, not just for their future relationships, but also for their protection and success.

15. Romantic Love

Young children often do not fully understand the concept of romantic love. It might be confusing to them that saying "I love you" means something different depending on who's saying it to whom. Use this lesson to help them understand the difference and why it's important.

Start the Conversation

It's important to teach your kids that there's a difference between romantic love and the love you have for a friend or family member. First, define romantic love as appropriate for your family. Explain that love for family is usually tender, kind, and long-lasting. Teach that there is a difference between having love for a family member and "falling in love" romantically. "Falling in love" can describe romantic feelings such as infatuation and wanting to be married to someone, but it can also include kindness and bonding. This romantic love can lead us to want to be married to someone.

You may address the fact that these romantic feelings are something they will feel when they are older. Describe how you felt when you first fell in love. If your child is old enough to understand, take a moment to explain that real love requires action, not just good feelings. Discuss some actions that show love (treating someone kindly, sacrificing, helping, listening, teaching, etc.). Talk about your experience loving someone enough that you wanted to spend the rest of your life with them.

 ROMANTIC LOVE: *A form of love that denotes intimacy and a strong desire for emotional connection with another person to whom one is generally also sexually attracted.*

Questions for Your Child

- What is romantic love? How is it different from other kinds of love?
- How do people show romantic love? When is it okay to show romantic love?
- How old should a person be when they show romantic love for someone?
- What does it mean to fall in love?
- Why is love so important?
- How do people act when they are in love?
- What are some ways we can show love in our family that are not romantic?

Sample Dialogue

Parent: It's okay to hug, kiss, and snuggle with Mom, Dad, or other family members. What about other people?

Parent: Who do we say "I love you" to? When does it mean something different?

> Teaching children how to build healthy relationships will enable them to recognize when a relationship is unhealthy, build healthy relationships, and allow them to help others to foster healthy relationships.

Additional Resources:

"How to Create Healthy Relationships" from Educate and Empower Kids
This lesson goes through several helpful methods that will help you teach your children what a healthy relationship should include and not include.

"Real Life Lessons Learned from Beauty and the Beast" from Educate and Empower Kids
This article makes some good points about the good and bad in media portrayals of romantic relationships, then lays out things you can teach your children to prepare for their own relationships in the future.

"Helping YOUNGER Kids (Ages 5-12) Shed Light on Fifty Shades Darker" from Educate and Empower Kids
This article highlights 10 super helpful discussions you can have with younger children about love, relationships, respect, intimacy, and more.

"Managing Big Emotions Through Self-Regulation" from Educate and Empower Kids
This lesson guides parents in discussing the differences between what media show versus healthier alternatives of dealing with anger, sadness, frustration, and fear.

16. Adults Who Care For You

There are many different kinds of families all over the world. Help your child understand that family members need each other. Tell your child why you love them and why you enjoy taking care of them and helping them in every way you can.

Ponder on some of the decisions and sacrifices you have made to provide a great life for your child. Think about the blessings and joy your child has brought to your life.

Start the Conversation

First, explain that children need adults to help learn new things and to do things they can't do for themselves yet. Talk about how your child has lots of adults in their lives who take care of them in different ways. Ask your child to name some adults in their life who help and teach them. Discuss how grandparents, teachers, aunts, uncles, or neighbors help them. Ask your child what things they learn from their teachers and others.

Ask your child to share what they see their parents do for them. Feel free to share some of the things you do as a parent that they may not see. Share some of the memorable ways adults cared for you and inspired you as a child.

Explain that not everyone has a mom and dad living at home with them. Explain that a family is still a family even if it looks different from your family.

> "God could not be everywhere so he created mothers."
>
> —JEWISH PROVERB

Questions for Your Child

- Who are your favorite people that take care of you?
- What do they do to show that they care about you?
- How can you show love and appreciation for all that Mom and Dad do for you?
- Families teach us many things. When you grow up, what would you like your family to be like? How will you take care of your kids when you are a parent?

Activity

Plan a family meeting with your child. Let them decide what you'll do, what needs to be talked about, and if you'll play any games or do any activities. It could look like having a picnic with finger painting, or talking about a dinosaur book. Show them that they are part of the family, and that what interests them is important to your family.

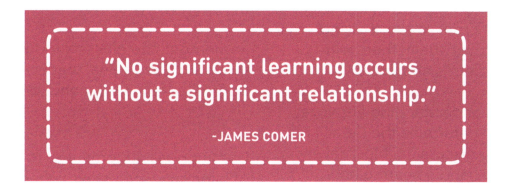

"No significant learning occurs without a significant relationship."

-JAMES COMER

Additional Resources:

"Five Great Ways to Bring Truly Open Communication to Your Home" from Educate and Empower Kids
Opening with a short, personal experience from the author, this article offers parents five ways that they can create and improve communication within the home.

"3 Ways to Improve Communication With Your Kids Now" from Educate and Empower Kids
The best way to show your child that you care about them is communicating with them in a way that they can understand. This article goes through a few methods on how to be a better communicator with your kids.

"Resolve to Make Family Time Your First Priority" from Educate and Empower Kids
Nothing shows your kids how important they are to you than actually showing them. Making time to spend together as a family will help greatly in showing your kids just that.

"Holding Family Meetings: A Necessity for Our Busy Families" from Educate and Empower Kids
It can be difficult to prioritize family time when there are so many other things that need accomplishing as well. Here is a guide on how to do that for even the busiest of families.

17. Where Do Babies Come From?

Many children know that women give birth to babies. If your child has questions concerning conception, gestation, and/or birth, answer them clearly and calmly, using correct terminology as applicable. Be sure you understand what the child's actual question is in order to avoid giving answers that overwhelm them with unnecessary details and vocabulary.

Let your own understanding and love for your child determine the detail and depth of your discussion. Most seven-year-olds can handle hearing how vaginal sex happens and how sperm and egg connect. Some six-year-olds are ready, and a few five-year-olds will be curious enough to ask specific questions like "how does the baby get in you, Mom?" or "how does Dad get the sperm to your egg?"

Remember, the glossary has helpful terms such as vagina, uterus, gestation, egg cell, pregnancy, penis, and more.

Start the Conversation

Use your best judgment as to what level of information your child needs and/or is ready for. You know your child, so you know what they're ready to hear. Begin by using words and terms they are familiar with in order to introduce them to new terms and concepts. By building off what they already know, children will have an easier time grasping what you are teaching them.

If you think your child is ready, describe the process of intercourse, how the sperm and egg connect, pregnancy, and childbirth. Feel free to use only the sections your child is ready for, and modify the following descriptions as you see fit.

A man places his erect penis into the vagina of a woman. As they move together, sperm is released from his penis into her vagina. When the man ejaculates, millions of sperm are propelled into the vagina. From there, the sperm swims through the vagina and the cervix and then up the fallopian tube. The first sperm to get through the egg cell wall will cause a reaction making it so no other sperm can enter. The fertilized egg is now an embryo. Within 24 hours of being fertilized, it quickly starts dividing into many cells. It keeps dividing as it moves slowly through the fallopian tube to the uterus. It then attaches to the lining of the uterus. This is called implantation. During pregnancy, the embryo, or fetus, grows and develops inside a woman's uterus. A full-term pregnancy lasts about 40 weeks.

Giving birth is the end of pregnancy where one or more babies leave the uterus by passing through the vagina, or by Cesarean section (C-section). If you think your child will understand a discussion of the gestational period, labor pain, cervix dilation, etc., feel free to educate your child on these as well.

Note: *Your child may not fully understand the first time you explain how egg and sperm connect or what happens during intercourse. That's okay. This is a lesson worth repeating!*

EGG CELL/OVUM: *The female reproductive cell, which, when fertilized by sperm, will eventually grow into an infant.*

SPERM: *The male reproductive cell, consisting of a head, midpiece, and tail. The head contains the genetic material, while the tail is used to propel the sperm as it travels towards the egg.*

UTERUS: *A major reproductive sex organ in the female body. The uterus is located in the lower half of the torso, just above the vagina. It is the site in which offspring are conceived and in which they gestate during pregnancy.*

Questions for Your Child

- Where did you come from? Where do you think babies come from?
- Do we know anyone right now who is pregnant?
- Would you like to see a picture of when your mom was pregnant with you?
- Babies are amazing! What babies do you know?
- How do you know if someone is pregnant? What does it mean when a person is pregnant?
- Human babies grow inside a mother's uterus until it is ready to be born. Where does a baby bird grow? Where does a baby kangaroo grow?

Sample Dialogue

Child: Where do mommies grow their babies?

Parent: Mommies have a special place in their tummies. It is called a "uterus." Babies grow inside the uterus until they are ready to be born.*

This is a very simple answer that defines terminology, but leaves out details of intercourse.

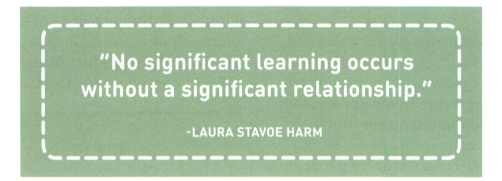

"No significant learning occurs without a significant relationship."

-LAURA STAVOE HARM

Additional Resources:

"Common Questions Kids Ask About Sex (And How to Answer)" from Educate and Empower Kids
This article gives some great tools about how to handle a child's curiosity about sex, and how to give honest and understandable answers to these questions.

"Common Mistakes Parents Make When Talking to Kids About Sex" from Educate and Empower Kids
This article goes through a few different mistakes and how to avoid them as you're starting out on these topics with your kids.

"Talking with Young Children about Sex" from Educate and Empower Kids
This article gives some great tips to explain sex simply and accurately.

"How to Overcome the Trepidations of Talking to Your Kids About Sex" from Educate and Empower Kids
This video goes through some of the fears you might have as a parent in having these conversations with your kids, and how to get through those in order to have productive and thoughtful sex talks with your kids.

18. We Change & Develop

Think about all the physical, emotional, intellectual, and social changes you experienced throughout your childhood. It's amazing how each of us grow little by little in each of these areas. This discussion is a great lead-in to talk about the opportunities we have to grow, learn, and help others throughout our lives.

Spend time listening to your child and allow them to tell you who they might be when they grow up. Children often imagine being a parent and/or a variety of jobs for their future selves, but they usually don't conceptualize the ways their bodies will change as they mature.

Start the Conversation

Remind your child that everyone physically grows up from being a kid, to a teenager, to an adult. If you have pictures from your childhood, show your kids how you changed over the years. Explain that changing and growing is natural and should be exciting and something we look forward to. Talk to your child about what changes they can look forward to. This will help prepare them for future adjustments such as puberty and the emotional changes that come with that, as well as growing bigger and taller and having more autonomy in the future.

You can also help your child visualize the changes their bodies will go through as they mature through a simple coloring activity. On a sheet of paper, draw three basic people-shaped outlines. Make the first one small, the second one medium, and the third one

PUBERTY: *A period or process through which children reach sexual maturity. Once a person has reached puberty, their body is capable of sexual reproduction.*

tall. Then, ask your child to help draw or color (depending on their ability) themselves as an infant, a child, and an adult. As you work together, ask them

"Ask any child development expert, and they will tell you that children do not develop in a straight line. There are no average children. There are no standard children."

—CASSI CLAUSEN

about their work and the choices they make. For example, "I see you've drawn a skirt on your grown up—are you going to wear skirts when you are a grown up? Why do you think you will do that?"

Questions for Your Child

- Q What do you want to be like when you grow up? Are there any grown-ups you want to be like when you are an adult?
- Q Everyone grows and changes. This is usually called puberty. What are some changes girls go through? What are some changes boys go through?
- Q Will your voice change? Will you be taller? Stronger? Wiser?
- Q Does every girl change the same way? Does every boy change the same way?
- Q What do you think your body will look like when you are a grownup?
- Q What parts of growing up are you excited about?
- Q Are there any parts of growing up that make you nervous, or that you are worried about? (Feel free to share some of the apprehensions you had as a child about puberty or other physical changes in your childhood.)

Activities

Find 3-7 photos of your child from their birth to now. While you show each of the photos to your child, share something new that your child was doing during that time in their life. For example, in a photo of your child at around one-year-old you may talk about how they were walking or climbing up furniture and getting into everything. You can even share some of your favorite things that your child said or did during those times.

Ask them what memories, if any, they have about the changes they have experienced in the past one to two years (starting a new school, learning a new skill, growing taller, etc.). Discuss how amazing our bodies are in their ability to grow, change, learn, and adapt to new experiences.

Find a place in your home to mark your child's height. Come back to it from time to time to show them how much they've grown. Each time you measure your child ask them what other changes they have experienced since the last time they were measured. Share what positive changes you have noticed in your child since the last measurement.

Additional Resources:

"Talking With Your Kids About Puberty: You Got This!" from Educate and Empower Kids
Part of the discussion with growing up will absolutely have to be about puberty. Every kid will go through it, so it will help with their stress about it if they're prepared and know that it's normal and natural.

"3 Strategies for Building Resilient Kids in the Digital Age" from Educate and Empower Kids
Along with your kids' bodies growing, so do their minds. Helping them learn how to be resilient to the dangers of a digital age will help immensely in their normal mental development as well.

"Daily Rituals that Can Bring Your Family Closer" from Educate and Empower Kids
This article goes through a few different ways to draw closer to your kids. Through activities like this, you can grow more comfortable increasing communication and comfort between you and your kids, assuring them that you're there to help them understand themselves and the world around them.

19. Other Words You've Heard

Kids will hear all kinds of references to sex and body parts throughout their lives. This may turn into a very giggly lesson! Talk with your children about what words are appropriate and not appropriate to say and use when talking about our bodies or other peoples' bodies. Help them understand why it's important to be respectful of our own and other people's bodies by being kind and referring to all of our parts with the correct names. Teach by your example! If you don't want your children using certain words, then you should refrain from using them as well.

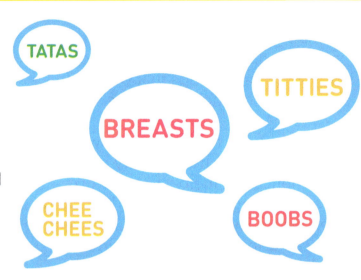

Start the Conversation

Depending on the age and past experiences of your child, it's possible that they will not necessarily have heard other words for one or more of these body parts. It is also possible that they will have heard many words for one or more of these body parts, and that they will find these words embarrassing or very funny.

Decide beforehand how your family wants to refer to these body parts and help your child understand which terms are appropriate and which terms are inappropriate. Help your child see the practicality of using correct terminology.

Explain that sometimes people use other words for body parts. Sometimes they may say these words as a joke. But sometimes they may use these words to insult others or hurt their feelings. Ask your child: why is it a good idea to use correct terms like "breasts," "penis," or "vagina"? This may also be a good time to discuss swear words or other slang that you consider inappropriate in your home. Explain why some words are offensive or hurtful, such as racial slurs, sexist remarks, or profanity.

Questions for Your Child

- Sometimes people are embarrassed by the words "penis" or "vagina." Why should we NOT be embarrassed by these words?
- Sometimes people use silly words to talk about their private parts. Is it okay to use fake names when we talk about our body parts? Why or why not?
- What are some other words for penis?
- What are some other words for vagina?
- What are some other words for breasts?
- What are some other words for one's bottom?
- What rules should our family have about body part names and inappropriate words?

Sample Dialogue

Child: I've heard breasts called boobies, titties, and hooties. *(Giggles)*

Parent: Some of those words sound pretty funny, don't they? But in our family, we are going to call them "breasts." Let's practice that word!

Child & Parent: Breasts. Breasts! Breasts!
(Likely more giggling)

Parent: Wow! You can say "breasts" really well! That is the word we use in our family.

> "Slang or euphemisms … may confuse the child and inherently undermine your message that it is okay to actually talk about this stuff."
>
> —JULIA BERNARDS

Additional Resources:

"Translating Slang for Parents" from Educate and Empower Kids
This article lists some terms commonly used on the internet and what they mean, to inform you of what people online might be saying to your child.

"Commonly Used Emojis That Every Parent Should Know" from Educate and Empower Kids
Similar to the above article, this lists specifically emojis and what they can represent online.

"5 Basic Tips for Talking to Your Child About Sex" From Educate and Empower Kids
When it comes to talking to your child about sex, sometimes just starting the conversation can be the hardest part. Here are some beginner tips to start you off.

20. Discovering Our Own Bodies

Discovery and exploration are a natural and instinctive part of development for kids. They want to look, touch, and interact with their world as they learn, and this includes their own bodies. This is the perfect time in our children's lives to teach them what is appropriate exploration and what is not.

Many children begin masturbating at this young age for the simple reason that it feels good. Typically they don't know that it's a sexual behavior and aren't intending for it to be one, but it's normal for parents to worry when very young children start. Simply redirect the behavior to another activity, but be careful not to embarrass or shame your child.

Start the Conversation

As a parent, you will need to determine what levels of exploration are appropriate in your family. Children are naturally curious, and it is both normal and healthy for children to explore their bodies in a variety of ways. You may wish to provide some ground rules such as "we don't touch our private parts around other people" or "we can talk about our bodies with our parents, but not with our teachers." Adapt any ground rules to fit the actual needs and concerns of your family and your child.

Additionally, this discussion can provide an excellent transition into a more detailed discussion about how our bodies work. Consider purchasing or checking out from the library a children's anatomy book to read with your child as a follow-up to this discussion.

Questions for Your Child

- Are you curious about your body? How can you get to know your body?
- Do you have any questions about your body?
- What are some amazing things our bodies do?
- What is something that you love to do? (Play outside, draw, sing, etc.)
- What is your favorite part of your body?
- What do we do to take care of our bodies?
- What is something you can't do that you wish to learn? (Cartwheel, splits, rollerskate, cross your eyes, curl your tongue, raise your eyebrows, etc.)
- What can we do to help you learn that skill?
- Our bodies are amazing and have many abilities. Is there something about your body that you don't understand, but are curious about?

Activities

Play "Simon Says" with your child! Help your child discover something their body can do, such as jump, sit, spin, or make silly faces. Be creative!

Song: Sing or read out loud "Do As I'm Doing" with your child. Mom and Dad, share some of the amazing things you discovered about your body as you were growing up.

Do as I'm doing;
Follow, follow me!
Do as I'm doing;
Follow, follow me!
If I do it high or low,
If I do it fast or slow,
Do as I'm doing;
Follow, follow me!
Do as I'm doing;
Follow, follow me!
(Pick an action you want mimicked and sing the song!)

Additional Resources:

"This Expert Says to Teach THIS to Your Three Year Old NOW" from Educate and Empower Kids
One of the most important things you can empower your children with is the knowledge of their own bodies, how they work, and how to keep them safe. This article gives a few tips on how to do this with your young children.

"Why Do We Fear Talking With Our Kids About Sex? … And What You Can Do About It" from Educate and Empower Kids
This article breaks down some of the reasons it could feel uncomfortable or scary to have such talks with our kids, and how to get past them.

"Talking with Our Kids about Masturbation—Without Shame!" from Educate and Empower Kids
Learn about how detrimental it can be to bring shame into any conversation about sex and our bodies, and how to address this tricky subject without it.

21. Affection

Peer relationships are a longtime learning process for our children. There are several essential skills they need to master. They need to learn how to play with others, show affection, but also protect themselves and include others. Through repeated practice, and trial and error, help your child learn how to stop themselves from continuing a behavior that has ceased to be fun for their friends, and also how to ask someone else to stop such behavior.

Because of the power differential between kids and adults, it's worth noting that navigating peer relationships is a separate skill from that of their adult-child interactions.

Start the Conversation

Ask your child what kindness is. Allow your child to answer and then share your insight. Define affection as well. Come up with several scenarios where your child needs to decide how they will behave. Ask them what they will do in the following situations: sharing a toy at home, meeting a new child at school, helping with a sibling, or taking turns on the swings at the park, etc.

Then give some examples of various affection they might experience with

AFFECTION: *A feeling of liking or caring for something or someone. A type of love that surpasses general goodwill.*

FORCED AFFECTION: *Pressuring or forcing a child to give a hug, kiss, or any other form of physical affection when he does not have the desire to do so.*

peers. Ask your child how they want to respond to these behaviors. Then, shift the conversation so that your child may practice the following in order to prepare them to say "stop" clearly and confidently, even when they are in a situation where it might feel awkward or uncomfortable.

- ♛ How do you feel when ____ gives you a high five?

- ♛ How do you feel when ____ shares a toy with you?

- ♛ How do you feel when ____ gives you a hug?

Questions for Your Child

- Q What are some ways you can show kindness to others?
- Q How do we show affection to our friends?
- Q What is the difference between playing and hitting someone?
- Q Sometimes playing crosses a line and stops being fun. Is it okay to say "stop" if it's not fun anymore?
- Q Is there anyone at school that it is difficult to be kind to?
- Q What can you do when others aren't being kind?
- Q Are you still friends if you say you want to stop playing a certain game?
- Q Is it okay to leave people out if they are different from you?
- Q What can you do if someone is mean to you or to your friend over and over again?

Teach your child that they are in charge of their own body, and to speak up if they are uncomfortable with something.

Sample Dialogue
(for your child to practice)

    Child: Please STOP tickling me; it is not fun anymore.

    Child: You may not hit me. STOP hitting me.

    Child: I do not want to wrestle anymore. Let's STOP.

Additionally, children should learn to show affection in good and appropriate ways. Help your child to understand that affection can be positive and help people to feel good about themselves when it is appropriately shared.

Additional Resources:

"Bodily Integrity: Teaching Your Child to Make the Best Choices for His or Her Body" from Educate and Empower Kids
Having body integrity is useful in so many regards including body image and how to protect yourself. It is also crucial in interpersonal relationships for kids to understand what kinds of affection they are comfortable or uncomfortable with, or what is appropriate to do with their bodies.

"Kids and 'Affection': Why I'm NOT Teaching My Kids To Be Polite" from Educate and Empower Kids
This article briefly goes into the author's personal experience of abuse, and how she decided to teach her kids about affection. One of the points made is about if a child should not be forced to be affectionate if it makes them uncomfortable.

"Talking with Young Children about Sex" from Educate and Empower Kids
This article gives a few pointers on how to approach this subject with young children, and provides useful tips such as what points to remember, simplified definitions, etc.

"How To Raise A Bully" from Educate and Empower Kids
This article goes through a few things that can lead to a child learning the wrong things and becoming a bully, often without meaning to. It goes into how to avoid these things to teach children how to be kind and considerate of others they interact with.

22. Play

Mr. Fred Rogers said, "Play is often talked about as if it were a relief from serious learning. But for children, play is serious learning." This is why it's important that we provide some structured play for our children, and lots of unstructured play away from screens each day.

Empower your child by teaching them that gender or what other people think should not determine the toys or activities they like. Children should be able to play with/do activities that they enjoy.

This lesson also works well with lesson #23, "How Are Boys and Girls Alike?"

Start the Conversation
Ask your child: When you have a friend, how can you be nice to them? There are no right or wrong answers in this discussion. The point behind this discussion is to start thinking about gender and gender roles. From a very early

GENDER: *Masculinity and femininity are differentiated through a range of characteristics known as "gender." However, use of this term may include biological sex (being male or female), social roles based upon biological sex, and/or one's subjective experience and understanding of their own gender identity.*

GENDER ROLE: *The commonly perceived pattern of masculine or feminine behavior as defined by an individual's culture and/or upbringing.*

GENDER STEREOTYPES: *A generalized thought or understanding applied to either males or females (or other gender identities) that may or may not correspond with reality. "Men don't cry" or "women are weak" are examples of inaccurate gender stereotypes.*

age, children learn to read social coding regarding what is appropriate for girls and what is appropriate for boys in terms of clothing, personal appearance, toys, colors, etc.

Questions for Your Child

- What are some of your favorite toys to play with? What are your favorite games?
- Do you think there are different toys for boys and girls? Why?
- Do you think there should be "toys for boys" and "toys for girls"?
- Have you ever felt like there was a toy you couldn't play with?
- Are there games or other things that are "just for boys" or "just for girls"?

Activity

Hold a playtime with your child in which you deliberately introduce toys commonly associated with the opposite gender.

Additional Resources:

"An Hour of Play Every Day: 77 Things to do Outside!" from Educate and Empower Kids
This article gives good ideas on what kind of games to play that are helpful for development and interaction.

"The Danger With Using Screens As a Digital Pacifier" from Educate and Empower Kids
"In the digital age where we are surrounded by screens it is important that parents take a step back and ask themselves if we're using these screens as an emotional crutch for our children."

23. How Are Boys & Girls Alike?

With the changes in the past few years of how we perceive gender and gender roles, much of the discussion has been divisive. Use this lesson to plant seeds of unity between your sons and daughters. Help them see the value in their own gender and in the opposite gender.

Start the Conversation

In your discussion, ask your family members to name as many ways boys and girls are alike as they can. Some of these might include similar histories (we all start out as babies, we learn, we

grow, etc.), similar needs (we all need food and water, we all want to be loved and have friends), and similar goals (to be successful, to have opportunities to learn and work, etc.).

Consider shifting the conversation to emotions and intellect. Both boys and girls can, for example, be happy, feel sad, be scared, laugh, cry, etc. Both girls and boys can write well, enjoy math, explore science, and pursue educational dreams. Emphasize the point that everyone, both boys and girls, has feelings, emotions, intelligence, fears, hopes, and special, individual gifts.

> By teaching our children to value all people, we must be prepared to judge less, respect more and advocate for a world where all humans, regardless of gender, are allowed to reach their full potential.

Questions for Your Child

- List things boys and girls have in common (two ears, eyes, hands, feet, legs, arms, one nose, mouth, heart, etc.)
- Why are there boys and girls in the world?
- What do boys do for the world?
- What do girls do for the world?
- What are some ways that boys and girls are different?
- Are there things that only girls and women can do?
- Are there things that only boys and men can do?

Activity

Invite your kids to play house and observe what kind of roles they slip into. After they are done, ask them what kinds of things they did, and talk about what kinds of jobs, chores, and roles can be done by boys and girls, or men and women.

> "Children learn as they play. Most importantly, in play children learn how to learn."
> —O. FRED DONALDSON

Additional Resources:

"Ways to Empower Children Regardless of Gender" from Educate and Empower Kids
This article goes through a few different on ideas how to teach feminism in it's true form to your children and how to empower them with the knowledge that they are unique and special whether they are a boy or a girl.

"Teaching Our Kids Body Gratitude: A Critical Skill in Our Image-Saturated World" from Educate and Empower Kids
"We need to teach our [kids] to be confident, happy, and self-assured no matter what kind of body they are living in."

"Understanding Gender Identity Terminology: A Guide for Parents" from Educate and Empower Kids
"Whether you agree with the idea of choosing one's gender or not, it is helpful for every parent to keep up with the concerns, trends, and shifts in societal norms and language."

"Parents: Use the Power of Response Questions" from Educate and Empower Kids
This article provides helpful tips for parents on how to use response questions: what they are and how they can help you simply and effectively answer your child's questions.

24. Friendships

Friendship can serve as a critical foundation in a child's life. If your child is so blessed, they will have good friends that they can grow with. This lesson can be focused to help our children understand that we can have friends of both genders, that we need to show courtesy and respect to our friends-and others-and that there can be great benefits to including kids who are different from us or sometimes left out.

If you would like deeper discussions on friendships, respect, assertiveness, boundaries, as well as topics related to our intellectual, spiritual, physical, and emotional "accounts," check out our book *30 Days to a Stronger Child*.

Start the Conversation

Teach your child that they can always form friendships with both boys and girls. Talk about what you look for in a friend and then discuss the best part of having friends. Ask your child what they like to do with their friends, who their favorite friends are, and what makes them good friends.

Discuss one of the greatest tools to keeping friends: apologizing. Share a time when you had to apologize and if necessary, practice saying, "I'm sorry" with your child.

Describe what it's like to be left out. If you have an experience of being left out as a child or teen, share it with your child. Ask them if they have ever felt left out and what they did about it. Explain that as you grow up, friendships can change or sometimes friendships

 FRIEND: *Someone with whom a person has a relationship of mutual affection and is typically closer than an associate or acquaintance.*

end. This can be sad, but sometimes friendships simply run their course. Teach your child that if they don't want to be friends with someone, they can (and must) at least respect each other.

Questions for Your Child

- Can you be friends with everyone you meet?
- Who are the girls that you are friends with?
- Who are the boys that you are friends with?
- How can you be a friend to others? (Sharing my toys, saying kind words, asking someone to come play with me, etc.)
- Can we be friends with people who are different from us? What if they are a different religion, or speak a different language?
- What is respect? How can you show respect to your friends? How do we respect someone if we don't want to be their friend?
- Is it okay if my friends make me uncomfortable or sad? Is it okay if I say things or do things that make them uncomfortable or sad?
- If something happens with my friends that makes me sad or uncomfortable, who can I talk to?

Activity

Tell your children about a friendship that was important to you during your childhood and how that impacted you throughout your life. Ask your child to talk about a friend they have at school, at church, or in the neighborhood that they enjoy being with.

> "It is vital that when educating our children's brains we do not neglect to educate their hearts."
>
> -DALAI LAMA

Additional Resources:

"For My Kids: The Perfect Garden or Online Friends and Face-to-Face Friends" from Educate and Empower Kids
This article makes a metaphor of life being a garden, with online friendships as flowers and in-person friendships as fruits and vegetables. There can be beauty in the flowers, but there is more substance to physical closeness.

"Lesson: Standing Up Against Bullying" from Educate and Empower Kids
This family night lesson is intended to help children learn to stand up for themselves and others around them when faced with bullying.

"Teach More Than 'Charity' This Season, Teach Your Kids Empathy!" from Educate and Empower Kids
One of the most important things children will learn through friendships is how to treat another person. This article gives some good tips on how to cultivate empathy in your children for all those future relationships.

25. My Body Poops & Pees

Everybody has bowel movements and everybody urinates. Remind your child that Mom, Dad, your teachers, Grandma and Grandpa, and even your goldfish goes potty! Going to the bathroom is normal and quite natural for everyone.

Children may require assistance in the bathroom, even after they have been potty trained. Discuss appropriate ways to ask for help, when they should ask for help, and be as specific as possible about whom they should ask for help from. Ask your child who they feel comfortable getting help from in each

In this lesson it is hoped that your child will avoid any feelings of self-consciousness in using the restroom, but also in knowing how to ask for help. This is also a good time to talk about any concerns you may have with your child in regard to using the bathroom or keeping themselves and the bathroom clean.

Start the Conversation
Just as teaching our kids that their vulva or penis is a private part, it is important that they learn to be protective of their bottom as well. This also includes being clean and careful when they use the bathroom.

URETHRA: *The tube that connects the urinary bladder to the urinary meatus (the orifice through which the urine exits the urethra tube). In males, the urethra runs down the penis and opens at the end of the penis. In females, the urethra is internal and opens between the clitoris and the vagina.*

specific situation your child might be in: preschool, play dates, church, with a babysitter, etc.

Accidents happen. Bedwetting is common among young children, even after they have been toilet trained. Nighttime bladder control often is not achieved until the age of six or seven. However, children can be understandably sensitive regarding bedwetting, even to the point of trying to hide the accident. Using the following discussion bullets, reassure your child that they will not be in trouble if they do have an accident and develop a plan for what to do if an accident does occur.

- Sometimes, we may wet the bed at night.
- Sometimes, we may wet our clothing.
- If you have an accident, who should you ask for help?

Questions for Your Child

- How can you keep your bottom clean after using the toilet? What can happen if you don't keep your bottom clean?

ANUS: *The external opening of the rectum, composed of two sphincters which control the exit of feces from the body.*

- If you need help while going to the bathroom, what should you do?
- What do you do after you go to the bathroom? (wipe, wash hands, dry hands, etc.)
- If you have an accident, who can you ask for help at home? At school? At church?

Sample Dialogue

(for child to practice)

Child: I need help wiping after I poop. Aunt Cindy, can you help me?

Child: I need help pulling up my pants. Dad, can you help me?

Additional Resources:

Everyone Poops by Taro Gomi
A simple, straightforward book for children that discusses how every person, animal, and insect on earth does, indeed, poop.

26. Pornography

Unfortunately, it's never too early to start talking about online dangers such as pornography and other sexually explicit content. Because pornography is a prevalent part of modern popular culture, children are exposed to it at younger and younger ages. Children's brains are simply not equipped to deal with the obscene, sometimes violent images of pornography.

Please keep in mind, you are not stealing a child's innocence by teaching them about the dangers of pornography. You are empowering them with knowledge. It is always better for your child to be prepared, rather than to feel scared of what may or may not be.

As a parent, you will need to determine when and where your child may be exposed to pornography and how to prevent such exposure for as long as possible. Ensure that appropriate filters are in place on ALL internet-enabled devices in your home. Avoid giving smartphones to children of all ages (even teenagers).

Note: Provide a positive, compassionate environment in your home as you prepare and discuss this lesson. Share your thoughts and feelings with your children. Remind your child that they will make mistakes in life—and that you will keep loving them, no matter what. You may also wish to talk about this lesson in conjunction lesson #28, "Pictures."

For simple, excellent advice on how to approach this topic further, check out our book, *How to Talk to Your Kids About Pornography*.

Start the Conversation

First define pornography for your child. Pornography is pictures or videos of people with little or no clothes on. These pictures and videos show private actions in order to make money.

Ask your child if he or she has ever seen pornography. Share your family standards and rules about pornography. Explain that there is nothing wrong with being curious about the human body; it's natural and appropriate. But pornography is not a healthy way to find answers about the body or sex.

Talk about how kids often want to show their friends when they have discovered something new. This unfortunately includes pornography. Teach your child that if someone tries to show them porn, that they can get away from them. Remind them, no one should make you look at pictures or videos that make you feel uncomfortable.

Discuss ways to get away from situations where someone is trying to show your child pornography. Read "Teach Your Kids to R.U.N. from Pornography" from the Educate and Empower Kids website to talk about the **RUN PLAN**. Here is a summary:

Recognize what you've seen and get away from it

Understand what you've seen and talk about how it made you feel with a trusted adult

Never seek it out again

Talk about various places where your child may be exposed: the school bus, sleepovers, camp, recess, in the classroom, at a relative's house, etc. Present your child with a specific scenario with a specific friend or relative. (Example: You are at your friend Maddy's house. She shows you a video with naked people on her tablet. What can you do to get away?) Discuss ways to get out of the situation. Consider having a "safe word" your child can tell you, in person or over the phone, if they need help leaving the situation.

Questions for Your Child

- What is pornography? Why is it wrong to look at it?
- What should you do if you see a picture or video of someone naked?
- What should you do if someone tries to show you a picture or video of a naked person?

- Q What should you do if someone asks to see you naked or in your underwear?
- Q Have you ever seen pictures or videos of naked people?
- Q Where are some places we might see pornography? (on a smartphone, on a friend's tablet, on a home computer, etc.)

Activity
Talk about the importance of making good choices when deciding which videos, shows, books, or music to use. Discuss how watching, reading, or listening to positive media can give us good, happy feelings. Some media may make us feel nothing at all, and some may give us icky or negative feelings.

Share 3-4 songs from different musical genres. Ask your child what feelings they have after each song. Then ask the following questions:

- Q What is your favorite movie or tv show?
- Q What is your favorite book or song?
- Q What feelings do you have when reading your favorite book or watching your favorite movie?

Have you ever felt icky or sad feelings while watching a tv show or other video? Why might some songs, movies, or shows give you an icky feeling? What can you do when you feel this icky feeling?

What to Do if Your Child Has Been Exposed to Pornography

Despite one's best efforts, during this discussion it may become clear that your child has been exposed to pornography. If this is the case:

1. Don't overreact or shame your child.
2. Determine the severity and nature of what was seen. More sexually explicit or violent material may be traumatic for young children.
3. Ask your child: How did it make you feel when you saw it?
4. Deconstruct or take apart what they saw. Help your child to take apart what they saw and understand that such images are counterfeit and that they do not reflect reality.
5. Reassure your child that they are not in trouble for seeing pornography and that it is normal to be curious about bodies.
6. Formulate a plan. Decide as a family what to do if confronted with or tempted to look at porn. If your child is traumatized, starts to actively seek out pornographic content, or starts to imitate explicit sexual acts either alone or with other children, professional help may be needed.

> **The brain responds to porn like other addictive substances such as cocaine, heroin, and tobacco. Porn, like addictive drugs, releases dopamine without regulation ... Viewing pornography changes the users' beliefs and attitudes about themselves and others, affecting identity and relationship expectations.**

Additional Resources:

"A Lesson About Pornography- for ages 3-7" from Educate and Empower Kids
This is a simple family night lesson guide for parents about pornography that is tailored specifically for children ages three through seven.

"Preparing Yourself to Talk to Your Child about Porn" from Educate and Empower Kids
This article goes into some ideas on how to take action and prepare to educate your children on this difficult topic.

"Protecting Kids and Teaching Them to Use Tech for Good" from Educate and Empower Kids
In this short video, Dina Alexander shares ways that parents can educate their children about pornography and using technology to make the world a better place.

"8 Ways You Can Fight Porn Beyond Talking About It" from Educate and Empower Kids
Pornography has saturated our culture, from clothing to speech to racy TV shows to hard-core porn videos. We can talk about porn with our children in open and honest ways in order to curb its harmful effects, but did you realize there are ways you can fight porn beyond talking about it?

"Helping Young Children Avoid Porn Addiction" from Educate and Empower Kids
One of the most dangerous parts of pornography is how it so completely rewrites the brain. This article goes through the different ways it negatively affects the brain, and thus the relationships a person has with others and with self.

27. Pictures

As a parent, you have a responsibility to help protect your child from potential dangers that they do not yet comprehend. The ease and frequency with which pictures are produced within our society often gives any child the impression that all pictures are fun, happy, or good things. They do not comprehend the rapid way in which an inappropriate photograph may be spread via text messaging and the internet to a large, public audience. Determine what limitations, if any, you wish to place on picture taking and picture sharing, and explain them clearly to your child.

Start the Conversation

First talk about how it can be fun to take pictures, especially of a fun experience, vacation, or special occasion. If you have one, show your child a photograph of your wedding day, graduation day, or other momentous occasion. Tell your child about that day and the feelings that come into your heart as you look at that photo. This is a good way to demonstrate how pictures can be a good thing, especially when it comes to capturing special moments in our lives to share with others.

Explain that some people take photos of people when they shouldn't. Ask your child if they can think of a photo they should not take of someone else. Teach your child that we should never take pictures of ourselves naked-even if a friend asks and promises to delete it. Discuss why we should not take photos of other people without their permission. Remind your child that we should never look at naked pictures of other people either.

We must teach our children that they are much more than an object in a photo to be stared at or shared. They are worth more than a photo click.

Discuss with your child the different ways that taking pictures can be both good and bad. Be sure to connect this with viewing pictures as well, and how pictures, when used inappropriately, can make us uncomfortable, sad, or angry.

Questions for Your Child

- People take pictures all the time on their phones. When is it okay to take a picture of someone?
- When is it okay to have someone take a picture of you?
- Taking pictures can be fun! What are some good things and people we can take pictures of? When might taking pictures not be fun anymore?
- What should you do if a friend asks for an inappropriate photo of you? Or tries to show you a picture of something violent or with naked people in it?
- Why do kids sometimes want to show their friends pictures or videos of naked people?

Activities

Before beginning this activity, contact another trusted adult (spouse, grandparent, etc.) and arrange a time to call them on the phone as part of this activity. Give your child a camera, phone, or other device capable of taking pictures and let them take a few. If possible, take a few selfies with yourself and your child. Explain to them that pictures can be a fun way to express affection and closeness.

Next, text or email a photo of your child to the trusted adult you contacted earlier. Have the adult call the child on the phone and describe to them the picture that the child just sent them. Help the child see that sending pictures can happen quickly, and that other people can see the pictures they send. Reinforce the limitations your family has placed on taking and sharing pictures.

To help your child understand that this happens with both good and bad pictures, ask them:

- What kinds of pictures are ok to send?
- What kinds of pictures are not ok to send?
- What makes certain pictures "not ok" to send?

Another great learning experience is to have a picture scavenger hunt with your child in your home or around the neighborhood. You could challenge your child to find all the pictures of them as a baby, or you could choose a theme to hunt for (certain colors, certain people, travel experiences, etc.).

Additional Resources:

"5 Ways A Mother Can Develop Self-Worth In Her Son" from Educate and Empower Kids
This article offers mothers a variety of ways that they can help their sons develop positive self-worth.

"5 Things A Father Can Do to Increase His Daughter's Self-Worth" from Educate and Empower Kids
This article describes a number of ways that fathers can help their daughters to develop positive self-worth.

"I Love Myself and That's What Makes Me Beautiful" from Educate and Empower Kids
This article gives tips on how to love yourself and teach your children to learn to love themselves. Don't rely on others to do it for you!

"Empower Your Child Today Through Positive Self-Talk and Affirmations" from Educate and Empower Kids
You can nourish your child's view of themselves with a simple solution: compliment them! And teach them affirmations to help them realize their worth!

"Learning Positive Self-Talk" from Educate and Empower Kids
Children need to know that their self-worth is based on who they are, not how they fit into popular culture. This lesson can help you do just that!

28. Phones & The Internet

It can be quite difficult to keep on top of all the electronic devices in our homes, and how much time we and our kids are spending with them. It can be easy to think, "my child would never look at something like that," or "I'm sure our internet filters will catch every bad thing." The truth is, our children are curious and tech savvy, and our filters don't catch everything. This is why continual talks about safety and making wise media choices is crucial to their mental and emotional health.

Make sure that your child clearly understands what your family rules are and how they will be enforced. Our free ebook *Being Smart and Kind Online: A Parent's Guide to Internet Safety and Digital Citizenship* can guide in helping your family understand the most important aspects of internet safety, including creating clear rules and expectations.

Be proactive in talking with other parents too! Be up front with other parents regarding your family's policies. Ask other parents what their preferences are with regards to electronic content and devices. Even if another parent doesn't have your rules, by asking them about it you raise awareness and promote a culture of responsible media consumption.

Our book *Conversations with My Kids: 30 Essential Family Discussions for the Digital Age* was created to help you talk about smartphones, social media, and many other topics for our time.

Start the Conversation
Explain to your child that, although computers and

phones are great benefits in our lives, they can sometimes show dangerous content or completely waste our time. Teach your child that they should take any phone, tablet, etc., directly to a trusted adult if it begins to display images that make them uncomfortable. Remind your child of the "icky" feelings talked about in lesson #13, "Your Instincts Keep You Safe." Explain that, if they see something on an electronic device that gives them that icky feeling, they should come and tell you or another trusted adult immediately.

Be sure to reinforce this behavior in your children by praising them when they do bring something to you to show you—resist the temptation to get upset if they bring you something trivial or inconsequential. The important pattern to develop here is a pattern of trust. You want your child to trust you and turn to you when they encounter things that they don't understand or that are unsettling to them. Then, if they ever encounter something potentially harmful or dangerous, they will be much more likely to turn to you rather than hide.

> **As we work together with our children to be more physically active, create boundaries around our phones, and brainstorm for fun alternatives, we can create a healthy balance with technology in our families!**

Questions for Your Child

- What are some ways we can use technology for good?
- What are our family's rules about the internet and technology?
- What can you do at a friend's house if others are watching something inappropriate?
- What do your teachers say about using the internet and technology safely?
- What should you do when you see a bad picture on a phone, computer, or TV?
- In our house, when can we watch TV? When can we play on the computer or tablet?
- What movies are okay for us to watch at our house? At a friend's house?
- What should we do if our friends offer to let us use their phones or other electronics?
- What are some good things we can play or watch on phones or computers?

- Is there a way we can use phones or computers to help or show kindness to other people?
- What are some ways kids or grown-ups can use computers or other technology to make the world a better place?

Activity

Make a play phone with paper cups or cans and string, then have fun conversing through the toy. Afterwards, talk about the usefulness of being able to contact each other from long distances. Discuss favorite friends or relatives you enjoy talking to this way and ask your kids how it makes them feel to be able to do that.

Teach your child about the many things we can learn from the growing and changing technologies around us. Remind them that phones, computers, and other technology can be used to help others, and to create a better world to live in. We can reach out to experts through email and social media, and we can share useful information to friends and family through social media and text. We can be a voice of truth and goodness online and even have the opportunity to create new technology that inspires and leads to positive change.

Emphasize the good that phones can do, but also discuss the dangers and how to avoid them. The resources below and the information in lesson #11, "Predators," and lesson #26, "Pornography," will be helpful for this discussion.

Additional Resources:

Noah's New Phone: A Story about Using Technology for Good from Educate and Empower Kids
A great family night book featuring a poignant story that addresses smartphone rules, online bullying, social media, and more.

"Basic Tools for an Internet Enabled Family" from Educate and Empower Kids
This article goes through several tools and ideas on how to keep your family safe as the internet is used in your home.

"3 Tips for Replacing Phone Time with Family Time" from Educate and Empower Kids
There are many ways to engage as a family that don't include technology. This article lists a few ways you can encourage that with your children.

"Kid-Friendly Alternatives to Smartphones: Taking the Smart out of Smartphones" from Educate and Empower Kids
This article lists some alternatives to smartphones that will not allow for the access to the whole internet, but will allow us to contact our kids and know that they're safe at any given time.

A Family's Guide to Digital Media from Educate and Empower Kids
This guidebook was created to assist you and your family in finding a media balance by providing you the tools and information you need to create your own family media usage plan.

29. Nudity

Children are innocent, naive and generally think nothing of their own nudity. They even consider it to be funny sometimes. It's indeed common for young children to incorporate nudity into their imaginative play. They usually do not understand that their bodies are special and need to be protected. This is why it's important to help your child understand their worth and reinforce rules and boundaries in this regard.

At this young age, it is especially important that children develop a healthy sense of their own bodily integrity. As such, arbitrary rules regarding nudity such as "It is always bad to be naked" can cause unintentional damage by promoting an underlying sense of shame and even loathing with regards to the body.

Determine as a family what the appropriate boundaries regarding nudity are for your personal situation, and avoid associating shame with bodies. Be sure to clearly explain the "why" behind rules you set within your home regarding nudity.

> "The innocence of children is what makes them stand out as a shining example to the rest of the world."
>
> -KURT CHAMBERS

Start the Conversation

First, remind your child that their body is special, beautiful, and worth protecting. Share a time in your life when you were physically injured. Talk about how you healed, who helped you, and what you learned from that experience.

Point out that we have many things we use to protect our bodies such as seat belts, helmets, clothing, shoes, protective gloves, goggles, etc. Describe how important shoes and clothing are in helping us be comfortable, stay warm or cool, and stay safe. Remind your child that although our bodies are beautiful and good, we still need to protect our bodies by wearing clothes.

Then, explain how our society has certain rules and laws when it comes to nudity. Talk about the rules you have in your home regarding nudity. Should we only be naked in the bathroom or bedroom? Or can we be naked anywhere in our house? Do we need to knock on a door in case someone isn't dressed? Be specific so that your child can fully understand your expectations.

Questions for Your Child

- We have beautiful, special bodies. If our bodies are so beautiful, why do we need to cover them up with clothes?
- You are special and worth protecting, so you need to wear clothes. What makes your body special?
- Why is it okay to be naked in some places but not in other places?
- Wearing modest clothes applies to both boys and girls. How can you be modest in your dress?
- Is nudity okay in our house?
- What do we do if we accidentally see someone naked?
- Why is nudity okay in private? Why is nudity not okay in public?

Sample Dialogue

Parent: Sarah, please close the bathroom door. I am taking a shower and would like my privacy.

Child: I see your bum! Ha ha ha ha!

Parent: Sarah, I know bums can be funny, but some people don't like their bodies to be laughed at.

Additional Resources:

"Teaching Without Shame: Understanding Your Child's Curiosity" from Educate and Empower Kids
This article talks of the importance of distinguishing between pornography and art, and how to teach a young child that curiosity is normal, but they also need to be respectful of others' privacy as well.

"Be Your Child's First Choice for Sex Ed -Instead of Google" from Educate and Empower Kids
This article goes through some of the ways you can dissuade this impulse to google over having your kids ask you directly.

"How to Make Your Home a Safe Space" from Educate and Empower Kids
There are many different ways to make a space safe, be it physically, emotionally, etc. This article gives an overview of the different ways to do this, especially from online threats.

"Bodily Integrity: Teaching Your Child to Make the Best Choices for His or Her Body" from Educate and Empower Kids
This article offers parents a variety of tips on how they can teach their children to love and respect their own bodies in a culture that would demand otherwise

30. I Am Beautiful & Strong

As parents, we want so badly for our kids to be happy and to see themselves as the amazing humans we know they are. But with so many voices pulling and tugging at our children's attention and giving them a skewed version of what is beautiful, we have our work cut out for us. This is why it's important for us to constantly teach and reinforce what we know to be right and true, including our view of what true beauty and true strength is.

At this young age, we can help plant seeds that lead to deep roots of strong self-worth by teaching them two important principles. First, that we can and must appreciate the body that we have, especially all that it can do. Second, we can help them see that our outlooks on life, behavior, and intellect are always more important than our appearances.

Our books, *Messages About Me: Sydney's Story, A Girl's Journey to Healthy Body Image* and *Messages About Me: Wade's Story*, each have a great story, discussion questions, and activities to help you have deep, meaningful talks about positive body image and healthy self-worth.

Start the Conversation

Take this opportunity to reinforce your child's sense of self-worth and their own belief in their individual beauty. Discuss some of the intricate things our bodies can do that we often take for granted like our ability to sing, dance, talk, listen, learn, climb, laugh, pray, sleep, etc.

Next, ask your child what they think makes people strong. What makes them beautiful? They will most likely mention external qualities. Recognize and add to what they say. Help them to understand that although they have many physical attributes that are attractive and strong, that their internal strength and loveliness is what you appreciate most about them.

Ask your child what it means to be beautiful on the inside. Explain that a person's kindness and goodness can affect their beauty. Talk about the people that you both know that you think are beautiful on the inside. Then have them think of someone they love and admire, such as a grandparent, teacher, or friend. Point out the ways that that person is beautiful through the actions they take, the words they say, or the way they make your child feel loved and accepted.

Questions for Your Child

- What are some things that make you beautiful? What makes you strong?
- How can you show people that you are beautiful and strong?
- How can you help others know this?
- What talents or skills do you have?
- What are some things or people that you consider beautiful?
- Why do we like beautiful things?
- What are your favorite things that your body can do?

Activity

Read or Sing *"Head Shoulders Knees and Toes."* Actively point to each part of the body as you sing the words. Discuss how incredible our eyes, ears, brains, bones, muscles, and other body parts are. Feel free to sing the song more than once, saying the words faster and faster as you do.

*Head, shoulders, knees, and toes,
Knees and toes,
Knees and toes,
Head, shoulders, knees, and toes,
Eyes, ears, mouth, and nose.*

Talk about the unique gifts that our bodies give to us. Besides making us beautiful, our eyes, nose, mouths, hands, and other parts help us experience the world.

Additional Resources:

"5 Ways A Mother Can Develop Self-Worth In Her Son" from Educate and Empower Kids
"Mothers have a huge impact on their sons' emotional development. We can help them become healthy, productive, and secure men by promoting their sense of self-worth."

"Learning Positive Self-Talk" from Educate and Empower Kids
This family night lesson is a great start to help your kids understand the power of their internal dialogue.

"Healthy Body Image: Your Kids Deserve It!" from Educate and Empower Kids
This article includes great advice to help you teach your child to have a more positive body image.

"Teaching Our Kids Body Gratitude: A Critical Skill in Our Image-Saturated World" from Educate and Empower Kids
"The idea that thinness is the standard for beauty is everywhere! We need to teach our daughters to be confident, happy, and self-assured no matter what kind of body they are living in." Here are three things you can implement to help your child!

TOPIC CARDS

CUT OUT THESE TOPIC CARDS TO HELP YOU START TALKING!
Post one on your refrigerator to remind yourself,
or to let your kids know, of the upcoming discussion.

1. OUR AMAZING BODIES
- What can your body do?
- Why are our bodies special?
- Who does your body belong to?

2. MY BODY BELONGS TO ME
- Why does your body belong to you?
- I can share my toys, but will not share body
- What does the word boundary mean?

3. MALE ANATOMY
- Penis
- Testicle/Scrotum
- Anus
- What makes a boy different from a girl?

4. FEMALE ANATOMY
- Vagina
- Urethra
- Anus
- Nipples/Breast
- What makes a girl different from a boy?

5. RESPECTING OTHERS
- Everyone has value
- Everyone has boundaries
- These boundaries are different for everyone
- Even if you don't like someone's boundaries, you still respect them

6. PUBLIC
- What does the word "Public" mean?
- What are some things we do in public?
- What are some things we DO NOT do in public?

7. PRIVATE

- What does the word "Private" mean?
- What are some things we do in private?
- Where are private places we go?

8. CLOTHING

- What do we wear to the beach?
- What do we wear to the beach?
- One way we respect and protect our bodies is to wear appropriate clothing.

9. GOOD TOUCH

- One way we show people we care about them is through touch
- What kind of touch do you like best? Hugs? Kisses? High fives? Knuckles?
- Can you think of ways that other people or even animals express affection to each other?

10. BAD TOUCH

- We DO NOT allow people to touch us where our underwear covers.
- Parents help us wash our bodies.
- Doctors can examine you when a parent is there
- What should you do if someone touches you in a way that makes you feel uncomfortable?

11. PREDATORS

- Most people are good
- These are bad people:
  _____
  _____
  _____
- These are people we trust:
  _____
  _____
  _____

12. HOW TO SAY "NO"

- You can say NO to anyone
- When is it ok to say "No"?
- Practice saying and yelling "NO!"

13. YOUR INSTINCTS KEEP YOU SAFE

- What are instincts?
- What do instincts feel like?
- What does that "icky" feeling mean?
- Have you ever had that "icky" or scary feeling?

14. YOU HAVE FEELINGS & EMOTIONS THAT CONNECT YOU

- How do you know your family loves you?
- How do you know your friends like you?
- Tell me about these happy feelings.

15. ROMANTIC LOVE

- What is romantic love?
- How is it different from other kinds of love?
- How do people show romantic love?

16. ADULTS WHO CARE FOR YOU

- There are many adults who care for you.
- They care for you in different ways.
- How does your parent care for you?

17. WHERE DO BABIES COME FROM?

- A baby grows inside a woman's uterus
- (If ready) Describe how sperm ad egg connect
- (If ready) Describe birth
- (If ready) Define the word sex

18. WE CHANGE & DEVELOP

- We grow taller as we get older
- What are some other changes that happen to you?
- How do boys & girls look different as they get older?

19. OTHER WORDS YOU'VE HEARD

- What are some other words for penis?
- What are some other words for vagina?
- What are some other words for breasts?

20. DISCOVERING OUR OWN BODIES

- Are you curious about your body?
- How can you get to know your body?
- Do you have any questions about your body?

21. AFFECTION

- How do we show affection to our friends?
- What is the difference between playing and hitting someone?
- Sometimes playing crosses a line and stops being fun.
- Is it okay to say "stop" if it's not fun anymore?

22. PLAY

- Do you think there are different toys for boys and girls? Why?
- Do you think there should be "toys for boys" and "toys for girls"?
- Have you ever felt like there was a toy you couldn't play with?

23. HOW ARE BOYS AND GIRLS ALIKE?

- We all start out as babies.
- We all want to be loved and have friends.
- What are other ways boys and girls can be alike?

24. FRIENDSHIPS

- Who are your best friends?
- What makes them good friends?
- As you grow up, friendships can change.
- Is it possible for boys and girls to be friends?

25. MY BODY POOPS & PEES

- Everybody has bowel movements
- Everybody urinates
- If you need help while going to the bathroom, what should you do?
- Accidents can happen.

26. PORNOGRAPHY

- Pornography is pictures or videos of people with little or no clothes on.
- (If appropriate) They show private actions to make money.
- No one should make you look at pictures or videos that make you feel uncomfortable.
- What would you do if you saw a picture that made you uncomfortable?

27. PICTURES

- How many ways can you think of to take pictures in your house?
- People take pictures all the time on their phones.
- When is it okay to take a picture of someone?
- When is it okay to have someone take a picture of you?

28. PHONES AND THE INTERNET

- What is your favorite game to play on a computer, phone, etc?
- What should you do if your electronic device shows you pictures that make you uncomfortable?

29. NUDITY

- NUDE/NUDITY/NAKED
- Is nudity okay in our house?
- What do we do if we accidentally see someone naked?

30. I AM BEAUTIFUL & STRONG

- What makes something beautiful?
- What makes something strong?
- Can a person's "insides" be beautiful?
- How do you show people that you are beautiful & strong?

IF YOU ENJOYED THIS BOOK, PLEASE LEAVE A POSITIVE REVIEW ON AMAZON.COM

Be sure to check out our accompanying video series for this book at educateempowerkids.org

To view or download the additional resources listed at the end of each lesson, please follow the link in this QR code.

GLOSSARY

The following terms have been included to assist you as you prepare and hold discussions with your children regarding healthy sexuality and intimacy. The definitions are not intended for the child; rather, they are meant to clarify the concepts and terms for the adult. Some terms may not be appropriate for your child, given their age, circumstances, or your own family culture and values. Use your judgment to determine which terminology best meets your individual needs.

Abortion: An abortion is a procedure to end a pregnancy. It uses medicine and/or surgery to remove the embryo or fetus and placenta from the uterus.

Abstinence: The practice of not doing or having something that is wanted or enjoyable; the practice of abstaining from something.

Abuse: The improper usage or treatment of another person or entity, often to unfairly gain power and/or other benefit in the relationship.

Affection: A feeling of liking or caring for something or someone. A type of love that surpasses general goodwill.

AIDS: A sexually transmitted or bloodborne viral infection that causes immune deficiency.

Anal Sex: A form of intercourse that generally involves the insertion and thrusting of the erect penis into the anus and rectum for sexual pleasure.

Anus: The external opening of the rectum, composed of two sphincters which control the exit of feces from the body.

Appropriate: Suitable, proper, or fitting for a particular purpose, person, or circumstance.

Arousal (in regards to sexual activities): The physical and emotional response to sexual desire during or in anticipation of sexual activity. In men, this results in an erection. In women, arousal results in vaginal lubrication (wetness), engorgement of the external genitals (clitoris and labia), and enlargement of the vagina.

Birth Control: The practice of preventing unwanted pregnancies, especially by use of contraception. See also IUD, condom, contraceptive implant, and the pill.

Birth Control Shot: Commonly referred to as the birth control shot, Depo-Provera® is an injectable form of birth control. This contraceptive option is a shot that contains the hormone progesterone and is given on a regular schedule.

Bisexual: A sexual orientation in which one is attracted to both males and females.

Body Image: An individual's feelings regarding their own physical appearance, attractiveness, and/or sexuality. These feelings and opinions are often influenced by other people and media sources.

Bodily Integrity: The personal belief that our bodies, while crucial to our understanding of who we are, do not in themselves solely define our worth. The knowledge that our bodies are the storehouse of our humanity, and the sense that we esteem our bodies and we treat them accordingly. It is also defined as the right to autonomy and self-determination over one's own body.

Boundaries: The personal limits or guidelines that an individual forms in order to clearly identify what are reasonable and safe behaviors for others to engage in around him or her.

Bowel Movement: Also known as defecation, a bowel movement is the final act of digestion by which waste is eliminated from the body via the anus.

Breasts: Breasts contain mammary glands, which create the breast milk used to feed infants. Women develop breasts on their upper torso during puberty.

Child: A term often used in reference to individuals who are under the age of 18. This overlaps with the term "teen."

Circumcision: The surgical removal of foreskin from a baby's penis.

Chlamydia: A common sexually transmitted infection caused by the bacteria chlamydia trachomatis. It can affect the eyes and may cause damage to a woman's reproductive system.

Clitoris: A female sex organ visible at the front juncture of the labia minora above the opening of the urethra. The clitoris is the female's most sensitive erogenous zone.

Condom: A thin rubber covering that a man wears on his penis during sex in order to prevent a woman from becoming pregnant and/or to help prevent the spread of diseases.

Consent: Clear agreement or permission to do something. Consent must be given freely, without force or intimidation, while the person is fully conscious and cognizant of their present situation.

Contraceptive: A method, device, or medication that works to prevent pregnancy. Another name for birth control. See birth control, IUD, condom, or diaphragm.

Contraceptive Implant: A long-term birth control option for women. A contraceptive implant is a flexible plastic rod about the size of a matchstick that is placed under the skin of the upper arm.

Curiosity: The desire to learn or know more about something or someone.

Date Rape: A rape that is committed by someone with a person they have gone on a date with. The perpetrator uses physical force, psychological intimidation, and/or drugs or alcohol to force the victim to have sex either against their will or in a state in which they cannot give clear consent.

Degrade: To treat with contempt or disrespect.

Demean: To cause a severe loss in dignity or respect in another person.

Derogatory: An adjective that implies severe criticism or loss of respect.

Diaphragm (Contraceptive): A cervical barrier type of birth control made of a soft latex or silicone dome with a spring molded into the rim. The spring creates a seal against the walls of the vagina, preventing semen, including sperm, from entering the fallopian tubes.

Domestic Abuse/Domestic Violence: A pattern of abusive behavior in any relationship that is used by one partner to gain and/or maintain power and control over another in a domestic setting. It can be physical, sexual, emotional, economic, and/or psychological actions or threats of actions that harm another person. (From the Department of Justice.)

Double Standard: A rule or standard that is applied differently and/or unfairly to a person or distinct groups of people.

Egg Cell/Ovum: The female reproductive cell, which, when fertilized by sperm, will eventually grow into an infant.

Ejaculation: When a man reaches orgasm and semen is expelled from the penis.

Emotion: An emotion is a feeling such as happiness, love, fear, sadness, or anger, which can be caused by the situation that you are in or the people you are with.

Emotional Abuse: A form of abuse in which another person is subjected to behavior that can result in psychological trauma. Emotional abuse often occurs within relationships where there is a power imbalance.

Emotional Intimacy: A form of intimacy that displays a degree of closeness which focuses more on the emotional over the physical aspects of a relationship.

Epididymal Hypertension: A condition that results from prolonged sexual arousal in human males in which fluid congestion in the testicles occurs, often accompanied by testicular pain. The condition is temporary, and is also referred to as "blue balls."

Erection: When the penis becomes engorged/enlarged with blood, often as a result of sexual arousal.

Explicit: In reference to sexual content, "sexually explicit" is meant to signify that the content with such a warning will portray sexual content openly and clearly to the viewers.

Extortion: To obtain something through force or threats, particularly sex or money.

Family: A group consisting of parents and children living together in a household. The definition of family is constantly evolving, and every person can define family in a different way to encompass the relationships they share with people in their life. Over time one's family will change as one's life changes and the importance of family values and rituals deepen.

Female Arousal: The physiological responses to sexual desire during or in anticipation of sexual activity in women. This includes vaginal lubrication (wetness), engorgement of the external genitals (clitoris and labia), enlargement of the vagina, and dilation of the pupils.

Fertilize: The successful union between an egg (ovum) and a sperm, which normally occurs within the second portion of the fallopian tube, also known as the ampulla. The result of fertilization is a zygote (fertilized egg).

Forced Affection: Pressuring or forcing a child to give a hug, kiss, or any other form of physical affection when they do not have the desire to do so.

Foreskin: The fold of skin which covers the head (the glans) of the penis. Also called the prepuce.

Friend: Someone with whom a person has a relationship of mutual affection and is typically closer than an associate or acquaintance.

Gay: A slang term used to describe people who are sexually attracted to members of the same sex. The term "lesbian" is generally used when talking about women who are attracted to other women. Originally, the word "gay" meant "carefree"; its connection to sexual orientation developed during the latter half of the 20th century.

Gender: Masculinity and femininity are differentiated through a range of characteristics known as "gender." However, use of this term may include biological sex (being male or female), social roles based upon biological sex, and/or one's subjective experience and understanding of their own gender identity.

Gender Role: The commonly perceived pattern of masculine or feminine behavior as defined by an individual's culture and/or upbringing.

Gender Stereotypes: A generalized thought or understanding applied to either males or females (or other gender identities) that may or may not correspond with reality. "Men don't cry" or "women are weak" are examples of inaccurate gender stereotypes.

Gestation: The period of time when a person or animal is developing inside its mother's womb preparing to be born.

Gonorrhea: A sexually transmitted disease that affects both males and females, usually the rectum, throat, and/or urethra. It can also infect the cervix in females.

Grooming (Predatory): To prepare/train and/or desensitize someone, usually a child, with the intent of committing a sexual offense and/or harm.

Healthy Sexuality: Having the ability to express one's sexuality in ways that contribute positively to one's own self-esteem and relationships. Healthy sexuality includes approaching sexual relationships and interactions with mutual agreement and dignity. It must include mutual respect and a lack of fear, shame, or guilt and never include coercion or violence.

Hepatitis B: Hepatitis B (HBV) is an incurable disease which is most commonly spread through exposure to infected bodily fluids via unclean needles, unscreened blood, and/or sexual content. It can manifest as acute or chronic. The acute form can resolve itself in less than six months, but it will often turn chronic. The chronic form can persist in the body for a lifetime and lead to a number of serious illnesses including cirrhosis and liver cancer. The younger a person is exposed to HBV, the more likely it will become chronic.

Hepatitis C: Similarly transmitted to Hepatitis B, Hepatitis C attacks the liver. Though most individuals with Hepatitis C are asymptomatic, individuals who do develop symptoms typically show signs of yellowing skin and eyes, fatigue, and/or nausea.

Herpes: A series of diseases of the skin caused by the herpes virus which cause sores and inflammation of the skin. Type 1 viruses will manifest as cold sores on the lips or nose, while the type 2 viruses are sexually transmitted and specifically known as genital herpes. This causes painful sores on the genital area.

Heterosexual: Sexual orientation in which one is attracted to members of the opposite sex (males are attracted to females; females are attracted to males). See also, straight.

HIV: HIV (human immunodeficiency virus) is a virus that attacks the body's immune system. If not treated, it will turn into AIDS. It is incurable and will persist in the body for life. It is spread through infected bodily fluids and sexual contact.

Homosexual: Sexual orientation in which one is attracted to members of the same sex (males are attracted to males; females are attracted to females). See also gay or lesbian.

Hookup Sex: A form of casual sex in which sexual activity takes place outside the context of a committed relationship. The sex may be a one-time event, or an ongoing arrangement. In either case, the focus is generally on the physical enjoyment of sexual activity without an emotional involvement or commitment.

HPV: Human papillomavirus. It is the most common STD in the United States and can cause genital warts or cancer in about 10% of those infected. Anyone over age 10 can receive the vaccine for HPV.

Hymen: A membrane that partially closes the opening of the vagina and whose presence is traditionally taken to be a mark of virginity. However, it can often be broken before a woman has sex simply by being active, and sometimes it is not present at all.

Hyper-sexualized: To make extremely sexual; to emphasize the sexuality of. Often seen in media.

Instinct: An inherent response or inclination toward a particular behavior. An action or reaction that is performed without being based on prior experience.

Intercourse: Sexual activity, also known as coitus or copulation, that most commonly understood to refer to the insertion of the penis into the vagina (vaginal sex). It should be noted that there are a wide range of various sexual activities and the boundaries of what constitutes sexual intercourse are still under debate. See also, sex.

Intersex: An umbrella term used to refer to the rare phenomenom of an individual born with some mixture of both male and female reproductive anatomy. This can be very obvious with visibly deformed or underdeveloped reproductive organs, to something as subtle as alterations in the xy chromosomes. It's also possible for signs of intersex to not develop until later in life.

Intimacy: Generally, a feeling or form of significant closeness. There are four types of intimacy: physical intimacy (sensual proximity or touching), emotional intimacy (close connection resulting from trust and love), cognitive or intellectual intimacy (resulting from honest exchange of thoughts and ideas), and experiential intimacy (a connection that occurs while working together). Emotional and physical intimacy are often associated with sexual relationships, while intellectual and experiential intimacy are not. However, people can engage in a sexual experience that is devoid of intmacy.

IUD: A small, T-shaped device that is placed in the uterus to prevent pregnancy.

Labia: The inner and outer folds of the vulva on both sides of the vagina.

Lesbian: A word used to describe women who are sexually attracted to other women.

Lice (Pubic): A sexually transmitted sucking louse infesting the pubic region of the human body.

Love: A wide range of emotional interpersonal connections, feelings, and attitudes. Common forms include kinship or familial love, friendship, divine love (as demonstrated through worship), and sexual or romantic love. In biological terms, love is the attraction and bonding that functions to unite human beings and facilitate the social and sexual continuation of the species.

Masturbation: Self-stimulation of the genitals in order to produce sexual arousal, pleasure, and/or orgasm.

Media Literacy: The ability to study, interpret, and create messages in various media such as books, social media posts, online ads, movies, etc. It also includes understanding how to navigate being online, what to avoid, and what information to share and/or keep private.

Menstrual Cycle: The egg is released from ovaries through the fallopian tube into the uterus. Each month, a lining of blood and tissue build up in the uterus. When the egg is not fertilized, this lining is no longer needed and is shed from the body through the vagina. The cycle is roughly 28 days, but can vary between individuals. The bleeding lasts around 2-7 days. The menstrual cycle may be accompanied by cramping, breast tenderness, and emotional sensitivity.

Menstrual Period: A discharging of blood, secretions, and tissue debris from the uterus as it sheds its thickened lining (endometrium) approximately once per month in females who've reached a fertile age. This does not occur during pregnancy.

Misandry: Like misogyny, it is the hatred, aversion, hostility, or dislike of men or boys. Similarly, it also can appear in a single individual, or may also be manifest in broad cultural trends.

Misogyny: The hatred, aversion, hostility, or dislike of women or girls. Misogyny can appear in a single individual, or may also be manifest in broad cultural trends that undermine women's autonomy and value.

Molestation: Aggressive and persistent harassment, either psychological or physical, of a sexual manner.

Monogamy: A relationship in which a person has one partner at any one time.

Nipples: The circular, somewhat conical structure of tissue on the breast. The skin of the nipple and its surrounding areola are often several shades darker than that of the surrounding breast tissue. In women, the nipple delivers breast milk to infants.

Nocturnal Emissions: A spontaneous orgasm that occurs during sleep. Nocturnal emissions can occur in both males (ejaculation) and females (lubrication of the vagina). The term "wet dream" is often used to describe male nocturnal emissions.

Non-binary/Genderqueer: Non-binary or genderqueer is an umbrella term for gender identities that are neither male nor female—identities that are outside the gender binary. Non-binary identities fall under the transgender umbrella, since non-binary people typically identify with a gender that is different from their assigned sex.

Nudity: The state of not wearing any clothing. Full nudity denotes a complete absence of clothing, while partial nudity is a more ambiguous term, denoting the presence of an indeterminate amount of clothing.

Oral Sex: Sexual activity that involves stimulation of the genitals through the use of another person's mouth.

Orgasm: The rhythmic muscular contractions in the pelvic region that occur as a result of sexual stimulation, arousal, and activity during the sexual response cycle. Orgasms are characterized by a sudden release of built-up sexual tension and the resulting sexual pleasure.

Penis: The external, male sexual organ comprised of the shaft, foreskin, glans penis, and meatus. The penis contains the urethra, through which both urine and semen travel to exit the body.

Perception: A way of regarding, understanding, or interpreting something; a mental impression.

Period: The beginning of the menstrual cycle.

Physical Abuse: The improper physical treatment of another person with the intent to cause bodily harm, pain, or other suffering. Physical abuse is often employed to unfairly gain power or other benefit in the relationship.

The Pill: An oral contraceptive for women containing the hormones estrogen and progesterone or progesterone alone. This prevents ovulation, fertilization, or implantation of a fertilized ovum, causing temporary infertility.

Polyamory: The practice of engaging in multiple romantic (and typically sexual) relationships, with the agreement of all the people involved.

Pornography: The portrayal of explicit sexual content for the purpose of causing sexual arousal. In it, sex and bodies are commodified for the purpose of making a financial profit. It can be created in a variety of media contexts, including videos, photos, animation, books, and magazines. Its most lucrative means of distribution is through the internet. The industry that creates pornography is a sophisticated, corporatized, billion-dollar business.

Positive Self-Talk: Anything said to oneself for encouragement or motivation, such as phrases or mantras; also, one's ongoing internal conversation with oneself, like a running commentary, which influences how one feels and behaves.

(Sexual) Predator: Someone who seeks to obtain sexual contact/ pleasure from another through predatory and/or abusive behavior. The term is often used to describe the deceptive and coercive methods used by people who commit sex crimes with a victim.

Pregnancy: The common term used for gestation in humans. During pregnancy, the embryo or fetus grows and develops inside a woman's uterus.

Premature Ejaculation: When a man regularly reaches orgasm, during which semen is expelled from the penis, prior to or within one minute of the initiation of sexual activity.

Priapism: The technical term of a condition in which the erect penis does not return to flaccidity within four hours, despite the absence of physical or psychological sexual stimulation.

Private: Belonging to or for the use of a specific individual. Private and privacy denote a state of being alone, solitary, individual, exclusive, secret, personal, hidden, and confidential.

Psychological Abuse: A form of abuse where the abuser regularly uses a range of actions or words with the intent to manipulate, weaken, or confuse a person's thoughts. This distorts the victim's sense of self and harms their mental wellbeing. Psychological abuse often occurs within relationships in which there is a power imbalance.

Puberty: A period or process through which children reach sexual maturity. Once a person has reached puberty, their body is capable of sexual reproduction.

Public: Belonging to or for the use of all people in a specific area, or all people as a whole. Something that is public is common, shared, collective, communal, and widespread.

Queer: A historically derogatory term against people who were homosexual, that has been reclaimed by the LGBTQ+ community. It is also an umbrella term for sexual and gender minorities who are not heterosexual.

Rape: A sex crime in which the perpetrator forces another person to have sexual intercourse against their will and without consent. Rape often occurs through the threat or actuality of violence against the victim.

Rape Culture: A culture in which rape is pervasive and, to an extent, normalized due to cultural and societal attitudes towards gender and sexuality. Behaviors that facilitate rape culture include victim blaming, sexual objectification, and denial regarding sexual violence.

Relationship: The state of being connected, united, or related to another person.

Rhythm Method: A method of avoiding pregnancy by restricting sexual intercourse to the times of a woman's menstrual cycle when ovulation and conception are least likely to occur. Because it can be difficult to predict ovulation, the effectiveness of the rhythm method is on average just 75-87%.

Romantic Love: A form of love that denotes intimacy and a strong desire for emotional connection with another person to whom one is generally also sexually attracted.

Scrotum: The pouch of skin underneath the penis that contains the testicles.

Self-Worth/Self-Esteem: An individual's overall emotional evaluation of their own worth. Self-worth is both a judgment of the self and an attitude toward the self. More generally, the term is used to describe a confidence in one's own value or abilities.

Semen: The male reproductive fluid, which contains spermatozoa in suspension. Semen exits the penis through ejaculation.

Serial Monogamy: A mating system in which a man or woman can only form a long-term, committed relationship (such as marriage) with one partner at a time. Should the relationship dissolve, the individual may go on to form another relationship, but only after the first relationship has ceased.

Sex (Sexual Intercourse): Sexual activity, also known as coitus or copulation, which is most commonly understood to refer to the insertion of the penis into the vagina (vaginal sex). It should be noted that there are a wide range of various sexual activities and the boundaries of what constitutes sexual intercourse are still under debate. See also, intercourse.

Sexting: The sending or distribution of sexually explicit images, messages, or other material via phones, email, or instant messaging.

Sexual Abuse: The improper sexual usage or treatment of another person, often to unfairly gain power or other benefit in the relationship. In instances of sexual abuse, undesired sexual behaviors are forced upon one person by another.

Sexual Assault: A term often used in legal contexts to refer to sexual violence. Sexual assault occurs when there is any non-consensual sexual contact or violence. Examples include rape, groping, forced kissing, child sexual abuse, and sexual torture.

Sexual Harassment: Harassment involving unwanted sexual advances or obscene remarks. Sexual harassment can be a form of sexual coercion as well as an undesired sexual proposition, including the promise of reward in exchange for sexual favors.

Sexual Identification: How one thinks of oneself in terms of whom one is romantically or sexually attracted to.

Shame: The painful feeling arising from the consciousness of something dishonorable, improper, ridiculous, etc., done by oneself or another.

Slut-shaming: The act of criticizing, attacking, or shaming a woman for her real or presumed sexual activity, or for behaving in ways that someone thinks are associated with her real or presumed sexual activity.

Sperm: The male reproductive cell, consisting of a head, midpiece, and tail. The head contains the genetic material, while the tail is used to propel the sperm as it travels towards the egg.

Spontaneous Erection: A penile erection that occurs as an automatic response to a variety of stimuli, some of which is sexual and some of which is physiological.

STD: An abbreviation that refers to sexually transmitted diseases, many of which persist in the body for life. These are illnesses that are communicable through sexual behaviors, including intercourse. Some of these illnesses can also be transmitted through contact with various bodily fluids.

STI: An abbreviation that refers to sexually transmitted infections. These are illnesses that are communicable through sexual behaviors, including intercourse. Some of these illnesses can be transmitted through blood contact. Not all STI's lead to a disease and become an STD.

Straight: A slang term for heterosexuality, a sexual orientation in which one is attracted to members of the opposite sex (males are attracted to females; females are attracted to males). See also, heterosexual.

Syphilis: Syphilis is an infection typically spread through sexual contact. It is a chronic, contagious, usually venereal and often congenital disease. If left untreated, syphilis can produce chancres, rashes, and systemic lesions in a clinical course with three stages continued over many years.

Test Touch: Seemingly innocent touches by a predator or offender, such as a pat on the back or a squeeze on the arm, that are meant to normalize kids to being in physical contact with the predator. Test touches can quickly progress from these innocent touches to more dangerous and damaging ones.

Testicles: The male gonad, which is located inside the scrotum beneath the penis. The testicles are responsible for the production of sperm and androgens, primarily testosterone.

Transgender: A condition or state in which one's physical sex does not match one's perceived gender identity. A transgender individual may have been assigned a sex at birth based on their genitals, but feel that this assignation is false or incomplete. They also may be someone who does not wish to be identified by conventional gender roles and instead combines or moves between them (often referred to as gender-fluid).

Uncomfortable: Feeling or causing discomfort or unease; disquieting.

Under the Influence: Being physically affected by alcohol or drugs.

Urethra: The tube that connects the urinary bladder to the urinary meatus (the orifice through which the urine exits the urethra tube). In males, the urethra runs down the penis and opens at the end of the penis. In females, the urethra is internal and opens between the clitoris and the vagina.

Urination: The process through which urine is released from the urinary bladder to travel down the urethra and exit the body at the urinary meatus.

Uterus: A major reproductive sex organ in the female body. The uterus is located in the lower half of the torso, just above the vagina. It is the site in which offspring are conceived and in which they gestate during pregnancy.

Vagina: The muscular tube leading from the external genitals to the cervix of the uterus in women. During sexual intercourse, the penis can be inserted into the vagina. During childbirth, the infant exits the uterus through the vagina.

Vaginal Discharge/Secretions: Vaginal discharge is the umbrella term for the clear/milky white fluid that secretes from the vagina daily. This discharge is the means by which the vagina keeps itself clean by discharging cells and debris. When a woman is sexually aroused, she will see an increase in this secretion as a means of preparing the vagina for sex.

Vaginal Sex: A form of sexual intercourse in which the penis is inserted into the vagina.

Vaginismus: A medical condition in which a woman experiences pain from any form of vaginal penetration, including sexual intercourse, the use of tampons or menstrual cups, and/or gynecological examinations.

Victim: A person who is harmed, injured, or killed as the result of an accident or crime.

Virgin: A person, male or female, who has never engaged in sexual intercourse.

Vulva: The parts of the female sexual organs that are on the outside of the body.

Wet Dreams: A slang term for nocturnal emissions. A nocturnal emission is a spontaneous orgasm that occurs during sleep. Nocturnal emissions can occur in both males (ejaculation) and females (lubrication of the vagina).

CHECK OUT ALL OF OUR BOOKS AVAILABLE ON OUR WEBSITE AND AMAZON.COM

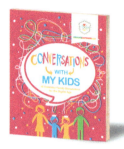

Conversations With My Kids: 30 Essential Family Discussions for the Digital Age

Parenting in the digital age has never been tougher. The world is changing faster than we can keep up with! It seems like there's always a new toy or device at every turn. With all this new tech, comes new information and new dangers. Our kids are exploring world issues and personal questions you and I didn't face at their age. Conversations With My Kids gives you the words and handy discussion questions to have meaningful talks about 30 very timely topics.

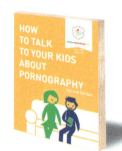

How to Talk to Your Kids About Pornography: 2nd Edition

Never before has it been so easy to talk with your children or teens about this tough topic. With smartphones and tablets everywhere, our kids are engaged in one of the most incredible social experiments ever conceived in the history of mankind. Within this alarming experiment, our children are becoming entrenched in an increasingly pornified culture. Take the time now to protect and prepare your family. Whether they are 6 or 16, you will have worthwhile, relevant discussions that will educate and prepare your family. Also available in Spanish.

30 Days of Sex Talks Empowering Your Child with Knowledge of Sexual Intimacy

Written by parents and reviewed by professionals, 30 Days of Sex Talks makes it simple for you and your child to talk about the mechanics of sex, emotional intimacy, healthy and abusive relationships, and so much more. We've broken down "the talk" into 30 uncomplicated "chats" to make it simple for you to engage in these critical conversations with your children. Remember, talking to your kids about healthy sexuality doesn't have to be awkward! It can be very empowering for you and your kids.

30 Days to a Stronger Child

As our families face an uncertain future, there are skills and qualities we must help our children develop in order for them to grow resilient, strong, and successful. That's why we've given you an engaging, straightforward way to teach the vital concepts of physical health, emotional strength, social skills, spiritual balance, and intellectual growth to your children. We've included activities, discussions, and questions that will empower you to raise a stronger, more exceptional child.

Petra's Power to See: A Media Literacy Adventure

We are surrounded by messages (media)--most of them are beautiful! Some inspire us to learn and grow, but some messages are empty and unhealthy. Join Petra and her dad as they venture into the city to learn about the powerful media messages all around us. They come face to face with clear and hidden messages in different media such as advertising, social media, and fake news. Petra and her dad will teach you what media is, how it affects us, and how to make wise choices when using media.

Noah's New Phone: A Story About Using Technology for Good

When Noah gets a smartphone for his birthday, he quickly realizes the power he holds in his hands. He becomes aware of its power to do good and inspire positive change as well as its negative and hurtful capacity. A great read-together book, Noah's New Phone also includes a handy workbook to reinforce important elements of the story like choices, safety, healthy boundaries and the huge potential within technology.

Messages About Me: Sydney's Story: A Girl's Journey to Healthy Body Image

Messages About Me: Wade's Story: A Boy's Quest for Healthy Body Image

Our kids receive hundreds, possibly thousands of messages every day from friends, family members, acquaintances, advertisements, social media, TV, and elsewhere. Join Sydney and Wade on their individual journeys as they first struggle and then, with the help of parents and a good friend, come to understand they are happy to be themselves and are truly beautiful the way they are.

Made in the USA
Las Vegas, NV
02 December 2024